Drama for Learning

Dorothy Heathcote's Mantle of the Expert Approach to Education

- Dorothy Heathcote
- Gavin Bolton

Dimensions of Drama
General editor: Cecily O'Neill

Heinemann
Portsmouth, NH

Heinemann
A division of Reed Elsevier Inc.
361 Hanover Street
Portsmouth, NH 03801-3912
Offices and agents throughout the world

Every effort has been made to contact the copyright holders for permission to reprint borrowed material where necessary. We regret any oversights that may have occurred and would be happy to rectify them in future printings of this work.

The authors wish to thank those who have generously given permission to reprint borrowed material:
    Chapter 4: *Monastery* by Marianne Heathcote. Used with permisson.

Library of Congress Cataloging-in-Publication Data
Heathcote, Dorothy.
    Drama for learning : Dorothy Heathcote's mantle of the expert approach to education / by Dorothy Heathcote and Gavin Bolton.
        p.   cm.
    ISBN 0-435-08643-X
    1. Drama in education.   I. Bolton, Gavin M. II. Title.
III. Title: Mantle of the expert.
PN3171.H326   1994
371.3-32—dc20   94-20582
                                                                                    CIP
Editor: Lisa A. Barnett
Production: J.B. Tranchemontagne
Text and cover design: Mary Cronin

Printed in the United States of America on acid-free paper
99 98 97 96 95 EB 1 2 3 4 5 6 7 8 9

Contents

Foreword

Dorothy Heathcote and Gavin Bolton, both innovative and influential educators, come together in this book to share, clarify, and extend their understanding of what is clearly a vital mode of learning. Although both authors are well known for their contributions to the field of drama in education, the implications of the kind of teaching described in this book go far beyond the concerns of teachers specializing in drama in education. Together, Heathcote and Bolton propose an approach to the curriculum that is purposeful, dialogic, emancipatory, and metaphoric. Students who don the mantle of the expert and its responsibilities are in an active state of attention to a range of projects and plans of action. They begin to generate their own knowing and, most significant, this knowing is always embedded in a fertile context. The mantle of the expert is essentially an approach to the whole curriculum, and one that resonates with current trends toward active learning and whole language. It is a rare example of truly integrative teaching.

In developing this highly articulated approach to the themes and materials of the curriculum, Dorothy Heathcote is proposing a paradox. The teaching is authentic, and yet it achieves its authenticity through "the big lie," since it operates within a powerful *imagined* context, created through the inner dramatic rules of time, space, role, and situation. This contextualization is the key to its effect. Thinking *from within* a situation immediately forces a different kind of thinking. Research has convincingly shown that the determining factor in children's ability to perform particular intellectual tasks is the context in which the task is embedded. In mantle of the expert, problems and challenges arise within a context that makes them both motivating and comprehensible. Imagination is not an optional extra to this way of thinking but is essential to the symbolic and communicative tasks that arise from the work. It is imagination that allows both teacher and students to devise alternative modes of action, alternative projects and solutions, and imagination is at the heart of this complex way of teaching.

Although mantle of the expert does not emphasize its dramatic roots, its purpose is the same as any effective theatre event. It engages the students both cognitively and affectively and requires them not merely to replay and repeat their existing understanding but to see the world afresh. Everything that takes place within the context of the work is elevated into significance. This significance is achieved through situation, role, and task, but above all through the language initially modeled by the teacher but claimed gradually by the students as their own. This "language" includes not just discussion but also written language and the reading and interpretation of a variety of sign systems. There is a growing sense of audience, both within the work and through the wider community to whom the students become accountable. Role play is an inadequate term for the kind of engagement required. The students inhabit their roles as experts in the enterprise with increasing conviction, complexity, and truth. They grow into their roles in a way that goes far beyond the functional as they experience the enlargement of both identity and capacity within the tasks they undertake and the challenges they encounter.

The significance of the social dimension of this kind of teaching should not be overlooked. Learning occurs most efficiently within a supportive and collaborative community. Here, students work in the kind of teams and collaborative environments that anticipate the challenges facing them in the real world. Instead of sterile competitiveness, everyone's level of achievement is elevated. The mantle of the expert sets up a supportive, interpretative, and reflective community through a pattern of relationships and a network of tasks, all embedded in a flexible context. Students are required to question, negotiate, compromise, take responsibility, cooperate, and collaborate, all in the service of something beyond themselves. Their energies are focused less on these interactions than on the tasks to be accomplished, and they develop an awareness of their own knowledge and competencies. They are active in the learning process, not just cognitively but socially and kinesthetically. They express their understanding in their response to the variety of tasks demanded of them, and they reflect on their perceptions from both inside and outside the context.

As Freire has shown, learners are motivated and empowered by the knowledge that they are learners. In mantle of the expert, responsibility for the learning is shared among the group and with the teacher. The teacher is also admitted as a member of the learning community, one whose commitment and courage, skills and understanding, are necessary to drive the experience forward. The key function of the teacher is to maintain the learning experience and support and challenge the students within it. As teachers work with this method, they will begin to understand more about their own learning processes; as a result they are likely to become more sensitive and knowledgeable about their students' ways of learning. All – successful learning depends on the capacity of the learner to bring relevant background and information to bear on a problem and to accumulate further experience as a result of encountering and resolving the problem. In mantle of the expert, the students' prior knowledge and experience is validated and their frame of reference is enlarged.

This approach challenges some basic ideas about the nature of teaching. Many educators recognize the flaws in our present approach to education—the multiplication of decontextualized "skills" and competencies, the obsession with measurement, the lack of challenge, the reliance on a transmission mode of teaching—practices that are visibly failing even where students themselves collude in these practices. Instead, Heathcote and Bolton share the assumption that education can go beyond the prepackaged, bite-size, fragmented, and highly disposable facts with which students' genuine appetite for knowledge is too often assuaged. The students are empowered not by giving them a spurious "freedom," but by encouraging them to accept constraints within which they will work to encounter challenges and take decisions from a position of increasing authority and knowledge. From the firm foundation provided by the teacher, the students gradually begin to take control of the imagined context, a control they have earned in a context they have helped to create. They *become* experts—experts at learning.

Bolton and Heathcote have much in common, although their backgrounds are very different. Heathcote left school at the age of fourteen without any formal qualifications. After working in a mill during World War II she trained as an actress. Her thinking has been shaped by her love of history, poetry, the Bible, and Shakespeare. Bolton's clear analysis of the processes of drama in education reflects his initial training as a teacher of English with mathematics as a subsidiary subject, and is elucidated in his many books and articles. Heathcote and Bolton taught drama in the Institutes of Education at universities within fifteen miles of each other and have worked extensively with students and teachers in schools. Their related philosophies have influenced educators throughout the world. Both are now retired, Heathcote from the University of Newcastle-upon-Tyne and Bolton from the University of Durham. But as this book demonstrates, both still view themselves as learners, and both continue to influence the field, through workshops, conferences, and writing. An archive at the University of Lancaster documents the work of Heathcote, and Bolton has established an archive tracing the development of drama in education at Durham University. Their work will continue to resonate in the authentic classrooms of the future. The partnership that began in discovering ways to enhance the skills of teachers has flowered in this remarkable analysis of a unique method that provides integrated and authentic occasions for learning.

Cecily O'Neill

Part One

An Exploration of the Mantle of the Expert Approach

Introduction

Dorothy Heathcote's and my careers have much in common in that for many years we held parallel teacher-education posts in the two universities in the north of England, at Newcastle-upon-Tyne and Durham respectively, some fifteen miles apart.

We were responsible for helping teachers and other interested professionals develop drama practice in a variety of educational contexts. Although a small percentage of our work was with student teachers, most of our time was spent enhancing the skills of *experienced* teachers—and sometimes actors, psychologists, psychiatric nurses, counselors, and (in Dorothy's case) people from industry. That our "students" were people well established in their professions had an enormous influence on the way we were able to approach our responsibilities. Our work became a *partnership* between tutor and student, a remarkable opportunity for honest exploration of the medium of drama and its potential for education. During those years our students helped us push the boundaries of dramatic expression in many directions. We learned a great deal about our subject, enough to realize that there remains a great deal to be learned. We hope this book will open up horizons for a new generation of teachers who will push those boundaries even further.

Although this book is jointly authored (sometimes, as in this introduction, it is quite clear which of us is writing, at other times we write as a composite voice) its purpose is to describe Dorothy's unique approach. Her students from all over the world have benefited from her methods and the time is ripe for making them accessible to others.

Dorothy has always been an innovator and has had an enormous influence on my own teaching. I can summarize some of the principles she has passed on to me:

- If you are in teacher education, you *must* continue to work *directly* with children, students in kindergarten, the elementary grades, junior high, and Senior High, indeed in educational institutions of all kinds, so that you are constantly practicing what you are asking others to do and evolving theoretical principles from that practice.

- Drama is about making significant meaning.
- Drama operates best when a whole class together shares that meaning making.
- The teacher's responsibility is to *empower* and the most useful way of doing this is for the teacher to play a facilitating role (i.e., the teacher operates from *within* the dramatic art, not outside it). The regular teacher/student relationship is laid aside for that of colleague/artists.

These four principles have become embedded in my teaching, so that I now find it difficult to remember working any other way. But, busy in my own university, for many years I was only vaguely aware that Dorothy was developing an advanced method of teaching built on these principles. Her sophisticated innovations in the use of drama challenged assumptions about the fundamental nature of knowledge, of education, of teacher responsibility, and of dramatic art. She gave this method (and the philosophy that goes with it) a name: she called it the *mantle of the expert*.

The mantle of the expert title seemed self-explanatory and from time to time I adopted it, or at least adopted what I thought "it" was! I picked up that "it" required that the participants should all play the role of some kind of expert, so I found myself telling students that they were social workers or the police or nurses and that they had to solve some problem in that role. Simple!

Of course, I should have known that Dorothy would not have wasted years experimenting with something simple! She is a pioneer in education dedicated to the task of finding the best possible form of education. This book is about that *best possible form of education.* In many ways it represents the journey I have taken in acquiring some understanding of this Mantle of the Expert approach.

It begins, in this introduction, with a description of my own somewhat limited attempt to use the method and Dorothy's subsequent criticisms. It continues in Chapter 1 with a dialogue between us about the essence of her ideas. This is followed in Chapter 2 by a brief attempt to lay down the educational rationale of the work. The remaining chapters give a variety of examples of planning for and using a mantle of the expert approach, examples drawn from Dorothy's past teaching, mainly in kindergartens and elementary and junior high schools in the United States and Canada.

. . . .

The book is about *education;* it describes how *theatre* can create an impetus for productive learning *across the whole curriculum.* A Mantle of the Expert approach is like a spiral, a continuous path followed by the students through *knowledge into theatre* and *theatre into knowledge* on a more and more sophisticated plane as they develop responsibility for their own learning.

I understand this now, but when I first contacted Dorothy about writing this book, I did not appreciate the revolutionary implications her method had for education.

My Attempt at a Mantle of the Expert Approach

During the year I taught at the University of Victoria (1989–1990), I wrote Dorothy a letter suggesting that she might consider writing a book with me about her mantle of the expert approach to the curriculum. I had an immediate reason for writing: I had just completed a fairly successful classroom session in a elementary school in British Columbia where I had used the second-grade students in role as experts. Although it seemed to have been a useful approach, I could not really appreciate why Dorothy seemed to use this method most of the time when she worked in schools and other institutions. (Indeed, I had heard of her highly successful work using this approach with top executives in industry!) To me, what I had done for one hour in a school in Victoria was effective enough, but limited. It occurred to me that perhaps what I had done fell short in some significant way of what Dorothy understood by mantle of the expert work. Hence my letter, to which she replied by return post that yes, she would be interested in jointly writing such a book—it needed to be done.

I then sent her a summary of my Canadian lesson. I had been asked to set up some drama in a school that was currently having problems with bullying, in particular the bad treatment by their peers of newcomers. Anyone in the school who did not wear "the right kind of clothes" or who had a "funny name" or a "funny accent" would suffer months of victimization, often of a cruel kind. The school had made a number of attempts to deal with the problem—counselors talked to the whole school, teachers tackled individual offenders, a special parents' committee was formed. But little change in the children's behavior had been observed, and part of the fun for the students had now become to continue the game without getting caught by the teachers.

My intention was to avoid making the theme of my drama session explicit to the children (their defenses against teacher moralizing would be raised straightaway). That it was about bullying had to *emerge* for the children as they worked at identifying some evidence. I had asked the class teacher if she wanted me to take a relevant theme from literature, but she said she would prefer me to tackle the problem more directly, since she had recently tried, to little apparent effect, using a story with a "bullying" theme.

So the context had to be a school, a fictitious one of course. The first step for the class was to invent a fictitious name. I put myself in role as the school principal, who failed to recognize that he had a bullying problem on his hands. I invented a boy called Melvyn (after making sure there was no child with that name in the class) who had recently emigrated from England to Canada and who, after a few weeks' attendance at his new school, had started to play truant. I invited the class in their role as "experts who give advice to schools" to examine the problem by interviewing Melvyn and any other characters they felt were relevant.

I decided that if the students were to concentrate on their function as expert advisers, *all* the other fictitious roles would have to be played by me. Therefore, I established the convention that whenever I was invited by them to sit on the interviewee chair, I could be whoever they wanted me to be. (It was interesting that they had no problem when it came to my playing Melvyn's mother—change of gender was just a logical part of the convention.)

The introductory part of the lesson included some questions that established the drama "contract":

1. I've invented a story about a boy called Melvyn—he won't go to school. The school and his parents don't know what to do about it. Do you think you could be in this story and be the kind of people a school calls on for advice?
2. Who will you want to see, do you think, in order to solve the problem? I realize you will want to see the principal of the school, but I'm not sure who else.
3. Can we agree that I can be any of the people you want to interview? If I'm to start off as the school principal, I'm going to need to know the name of my school; can we make one up?

The name of the fictitious school was written on the blackboard. I then proceeded to share with them (in my role as principal) this worrying truancy problem: "We've never had a case like this before in all my years at the school. Melvyn seemed to fit in very well the first week or so."

Once the students got over their initial embarrassment at asking questions of me in these various guises, they started to enjoy probing for details, particularly from Melvyn: What had he been up to while pretending to his parents that he had been attending school? Why, if there was no problem at school, as he maintained, would he choose to avoid it? When Melvyn continued to answer "Dunno" with a shrug, they questioned his mother and his class teacher, both of whom in their different ways claimed to be puzzled by the situation.

With this impasse the class began signaling some degree of frustration so I now introduced a sheaf of letters (reproduced on pages 9–14) that I said had been sent to me by Melvyn's grandmother still living in England. "These just arrived," I said in my role as school principal. "I don't know whether they will cast any light on the problem, but I've had enough copies made for each of you."

A buzz of excited talk in the room grew as individuals, having struggled to read the letters, gradually realized they were holding evidence of the cause of the problem in their hands. They immediately explained to me that they had "discovered" what had been going wrong, and they proceeded with a new sense of urgency to send again for Melvyn, Zach, and others. One expert badly wanted to interview Zach's mother to see why she had not invited Melvyn to her son's party. Although they did not use the word "bullying," their questions revealed some understanding of Melvyn's problem. However, when at the end of the lesson, as school principal, I asked them if they could give me some overall advice about avoiding this kind of incident in my school in the future, they were reluctant (or simply not ready) to generalize. Their concentration remained on Melvyn. I asked the class teacher as I was leaving if she would have them write a report on Melvyn's experience. Having to find the formal language for an official report is a valuable way for students to reflect on what they have understood and learned. Of course the real test would be whether there was any noticeable difference in their bullying behavior.

Having described this lesson (a bit more briefly than I've done here), I asked Dorothy, "Is this mantle of the expert?" I wasn't sure what I wanted her to say. If she confirmed that it was, I would shrug my shoulders and wonder what the big fuss was about. If she dismissed it, then I had a lot to learn and this book would get written!

Her answer? "No, it's not mantle of the expert." Not abruptly like that, of course; she even seemed to approve of what I had done "as far as it goes, in just [one] session." This book will be about what *more* there has to be in order for the work to become full-fledged mantle of the expert. We hope to take the reader through the very process I had to go through in order to grasp its complexities.

3 January

Dear Gran

Victoria is a luvley
place. I can see the
~~see~~ sea from my bedroom
window. I started B my
new school today its
great. My teacher is
Mrs Mark she is very nice
We sit in groups round our
desks. There are 3 children
at my table. I don't no
there names yet. They are
nice.

Take care of Fluss
Has she cort any more mice
Love
Melvyn

8 January

Dear Gran,

We had fun at school today. My frends names are Zach and Wayne and Tara and David. Zach got into trouble for throwing Pine Cones. I didn't throw any.

Please can you send me some proper runners for my birthday Gran

Love

Melvyn

15 January

Dear Gran

They laft at me in class today because I said a word wrong how was I to no

It was Zach's birthday ~~yst~~ yesterday he had a party I didn't go I watched them go into his house. Wayne and David and Tara were there.

Is Fluss o.k.

Love
Melvyn

26 January

Dear Gran

My mum was cross with
me to today my shirt
collar got torn I
couldnt help it. I
wish it was saturday

Melvyn

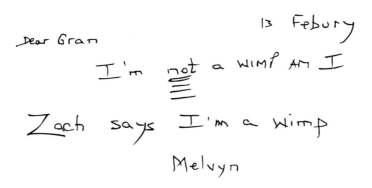

Dear Gran I hate school M.

14 Febury

A Dialogue Between Dorothy Heathcote and Gavin Bolton*

GB: So my bullying lesson wasn't really mantle of the expert?

DH: Not really. It's not enough just to give the students the *label* expert.

GB: But from the beginning of the role play they were treated as adults and their advice was sought.

DH: Yes, but you're still only sticking a label on them. It needs much more than that.

GB: But they grew into their expert roles as the lesson went on: they grasped the problem; they asked better questions; at least some of them did.

DH: What you were asking those eight-year-olds to do was quite sophisticated. Just list the skills you were requiring your class to employ:

- Asking probing questions
- Assessing responses, both verbal and nonverbal
- Reading between the lines of answers where truth was being withheld
- Recognizing why people (Melvyn, the staff, and perhaps the parents) needed to protect themselves
- Examining the letters to Gran for implications
- Sharing findings with each other and sifting them in order of importance
- Preparing questions to ask in the light of the new findings
- Getting Melvyn to tell the truth

* This dialogue is a recreation of Gavin's long discussions with Dorothy and of Dorothy's handwritten notes. It is not a verbatim transcript of a single conversation.

- Moving to generalizations about bullying and picturing other contexts to which the problem might apply
- Advising the school principal how to identify the signs of bullying
- Finding the formal and selective language of a written report.

No doubt one or two students demonstrated some skills not normally associated with second grade—your drama was putting them under pressure to work fast and come up with something. But for real learning to be going on, the students not only need to reinforce these skills through practice over a period of time, they need to be conscious of their new skills and concepts as they are acquiring them—that is, they have to *recognize* what they are learning—and they have to take responsibility at some stage for their own learning. A mantle of the expert approach can do all this—*and without members of the class falling into their traditional role of students/learners.*

GB: So if *you* were faced with the task of tackling the theme of bullying, what would you do?

DH: I would ask for several sessions—not just one.

GB: But that would not be acceptable to the school—to spend so much time on bullying, important as it was!

DH: Then the school would be missing the point about the mantle of the expert approach, which is always *an approach to the whole curriculum, not* a matter of isolating just one theme. Any one thing you want to teach *must* become meshed within broad curriculum knowledge and skills. So the five or six sessions in role as experts will not be confined to bullying (although this of course will turn out to be a critical learning area); the five or six sessions will cover many selected aspects of the curriculum: science, math, language, art, et cetera. Bullying will emerge when the time is ripe, that is, when the skills and knowledge needed to tackle bullying have already been harnessed in the carrying out of earlier tasks.

GB: You mean you delay bullying until they've practiced on some other—easier—task? So you would give them a different kind of school problem to deal with before the bullying one?

DH: I think I would probably want to broaden out the nature of their expertise in order to give them more scope and not seem to be tying everything to *schooling*. The students are more likely to take on the mantle if to begin with they are further away from a classroom-related situation: something more like a business where they are professionals who work as troubleshooters.

GB: When you say "a business," I get the impression that you already see a *place* in your mind, not just a group of potential advisers.

DH: That's right. A *place* where *action* occurs; where *tasks* are carried out with a high degree of responsibility. And these tasks would be carefully graded for degrees of difficulty. For instance an initial "contract" for the troubleshooters might have to do with redesigning an already crowded office space to take in an extra employee (lots of curriculum areas here), whereas a second or third step might be adapting the office work to accommodate a physically disadvantaged person (which of course would include investigating the limitations imposed by the handicap, thus moving nearer to interviewing Melvyn).

GB: So a mantle of the expert approach is a series of tasks relating to some *advising business.*

DH: Oh, not necessarily. In choosing "troubleshooters" I've merely paralleled *your* lesson, Gavin, in which you use the advising relationship. Instead we could be astronauts undergoing personality tests or designer/architects of a community home. The actual enterprise will not matter, because getting on with people in any work situation is a central social issue. My earlier suggestions about adjusting the space in an office or accommodating a person with some particular feature affecting work (blindness, for example, or extreme tallness) could still apply to astronauts or architects. The circumstances would vary with the context. Astronauts would already be space restricted, so in their case they might need to accommodate an extra piece of equipment or a person from another team: *accommodating to difference* lay at the heart of your bullying.

Regarding the contract—this is always about agreeing (a) to the particular context and (b) that "we shall run it." An advisory firm is only one of many types of establishments—those who *service* is another category your troubleshooting company could fit into. These are not the same type of establishment, nor would they develop along the same lines. Gas or water engineers, for instance, would for the most part be *servicing* rather than advising. The common ground is that each member of the establishment is a worker and functions within the team responsibilities, sharing in the overall aspirations and skills, and, in modern business parlance, subscribes to the mission statement of their firm.

Whichever we choose, we have to ensure that all the curriculum areas we want are accessible: I would want to include calculation, estimation, talk systems, writing of all kinds, reading, and perusing and there could be a historical, scientific, geographical or archae-ological bias, as the curriculum demanded. Obviously the trouble-shooting context is appropriate for a tricky social group—as you had with the bullying class—because I would want them eventually to sort out their own problem. Your lesson, of course, worked beauti-fully as a single session. A mantle of the expert approach would take longer and have a better chance of more healing in the long run.

GB: Yes, this is the crunch—does a different *quality* of learning take place when the ground is more thoroughly prepared and over a longer period?

DH: That's why we're writing this book!

GB: So, where do we begin? So far I'm hanging on to three aspects that I think I've understood. One: The specific thing you are setting out to teach *emerges* from curriculum tasks. Two: The students must be conscious of what they are learning, as they continually record and assess newly acquired knowledge and skills. And three: they must become *responsible* for what they learn, that is, *they* must make it happen. I am a long way from understanding *how* you do this, but let's stay with these principles or philosophy for the time being. Do you have any other philosophical observations?

DH: Plenty! I consider that mantle of the expert work becomes deep social (and sometimes personal) play because (a) students know they are contracting into fiction, (b) they understand the power they have within that fiction to direct, decide, and function, (c) the "spectator" in them must be awakened so that they perceive and enjoy the world of action and responsibility even as they function in it, and (d) they grow in expertise through the amazing range of conventions that must be harnessed, because if they are *makers* of things (for exam-ple, shoes, ballgowns, or aircraft) they *must never* (within the fiction, that is) *be asked to create the actual objects.* If they had to do this their *in*expertness would become immediately apparent. So *conven-tions* are used to avoid the authentic making. They in actuality *will* design, demonstrate, explain, draw to scale, or cut out templates *exactly as such firms would.* So in every way *except* making the actual life-size fabrication with authentic materials, the class will function as people sharing the work of the enterprise.

GB: As good little workers?

DH: Certainly not. There is no employer/employee division in man-tle of the expert kind of work. This system seems to me much closer to real play, which children invent for themselves and stop when they tire of it, than any of the fictional classroom dramas that lack the frame of "point of view."

GB: What do you mean: "frame of 'point of view'"?

DH: When you angle a camera before taking a photograph, the angle controls what is seen; it is a selected view that makes the entry into the picture (in drama, entry into the dramatic fiction) meaningful and disciplined.

GB: I have often heard you ask teachers, "Is there anything you always teach whatever you are teaching?" In the mantle of the expert approach is there something *you* are *always* teaching?

DH: In Dylan Thomas's *Under Milk Wood* there's a character of an undertaker who "measures with his eye the passers by for shrouds." This is what I call the undertaker's worldview—his professional eye is so deeply embedded in his life's value system that it controls the way he sees the world. It is such a view that putting on the mantle of the expert can develop in the students.

GB: Dorothy, if I tried to pass on to teachers what I think is the purpose of drama in schools, I would talk in terms of, one, a change in conceptual understanding, that is, grasping something new or anew; two, an improvement in life skills, including whole language; and three, a developing skill in using dramatic art form. Where do these three objectives stand in relation to your worldview?

DH: Your three categories may well be integral to mantle of the expert work at any time—but it's the deep immersion over a long time, leading to productive *obsession,* that I'd like to see developed much more. I'm thinking (in an ideal educational world—we've a long way to go) of a *year's work,* because like pleats in fabric, the work would develop by constantly evolving its future and then folding back on itself.

GB: I'm mystified!

DH: Five levels seems important to all social/cultural development [see the illustration in Figure 1-1]:

> One: I do a task, perform an **action.**
> Two: Because of a **motive.**
> Three: Therefore, my investment is in _____.
> Four: My **models** that have bred this investment are
>
> _____.
> Five: Because this is how life should be—my stance or **values.**

For example:

> Action: I pick up a piece of litter.
> Motive: To place it in the bin to conserve for other uses.
> **Investment**: We must distinguish at all times between useful and disposable materials.

The tasks always constitute the action through which the deepening levels become engaged.

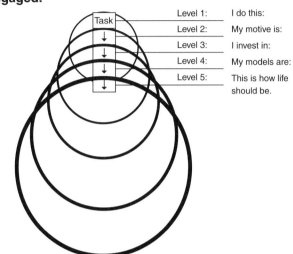

Level 1:	I do this:
Level 2:	My motive is:
Level 3:	I invest in:
Level 4:	My models are:
Level 5:	This is how life should be.

Thus the doing of tasks carries ever deeper meanings as individuals become ready to engage with the levels of commitment.

FIGURE 1-1. *Levels of Commitment in Social/Cultural Development.*

> Models: Experience, parental models (either to follow or contradict), the rules I approve of, or someone I admire or want to emulate does this.
> Values: My environment matters not only for me but for the rubbish itself, which now may be recycled. Nothing is to be regarded as useless. I am not so important that I can't serve the environment by picking up. This has become a worldview: this is what I am doing whatever I am doing.

GB: It seems to me that this model has a *static* quality about it, as though a person's psychology becomes fixed forever within a strait-jacket of: action/motive/investment/models/values. Presumably you are suggesting we all carry such a system around with us, including nine-year-old children who bully newcomers! Is their stance reflected something like this?

> Action: I am going to join in the teasing of Melvyn.
> Motive: I gain status at someone else's expense.
> Investment: I must make sure at all times that I am seen to be victimizing the "right" one.

Models: I learned this from the leaders I am anxious to impress.
Values: This is "how life is"—and no amount of moralizing by adults is going to change it.

And when we talk about learning through drama, therefore, are we saying that change can only begin to occur if the individuals concerned are somehow made aware of how this model operates in themselves?

DH: Yes, this is certainly true of mantle of the expert work. Let us look at how the teacher might make this model work for the troubleshooting firm:

Action: We put an extra cup on the office coffee tray.
Motive: So that everyone has a cup when it's break time.
Investment: People like to feel part of the group (or, cynically, as in your example above: it saves argument!).
Models: We are conforming with the notion of regular eating/drinking breaks.
Values: Workplaces give privileges and demand responsibilities.

Whether your classification, Gavin, into the three categories of conceptual understanding, development in life skills, and aesthetic development is relevant depends on whether the particular drama context offers the variety of individual response and levels of behavior that mantle of the expert can offer. The trouble with a lot of classroom drama is that there tends to be a strong group pressure to conform to whatever behavior or attitude has peer approval, whereas in mantle of the expert work, with its small-group autonomy and the absence of the usual kind of "teacher talk," the student's individual readiness is demonstrated. I can watch the five levels at which individuals are operating, using the above model, and service these different levels as they reveal themselves in the behaviors of different children.

GB: Are you saying there is something *hierarchical* about your list—that some students may be at the action level, some at motive, some at investment or models? In their own lives, they will be operating at all levels—however immaturely or unconsciously. So does it become hierarchical *when the students take on a role?* Which may *begin* with a child simply imitating the expected *actions* required and then moving to knowing *why* the actions are necessary and so on? Is this what you mean Dorothy?

DH: What you have done, Gavin, with your analysis of your bullying class, is to apply the model theoretically and generally to a *group* of children in a school where bullying was a feature. This is all right as far as it goes—and it's what we all do when we are preparing to meet a group of children we are not familiar with. But did you in fact use the model *diagnostically,* assessing where *individual* students stood *as they worked in role,* and did you then respond to each accordingly?

GB: I certainly did not use this model, but I would expect that I adapted, in some way, to what I read as individual needs.

DH: One would expect your general assumptions to be fairly accurate: the model suggests, quite rightly, an entrenched attitude to bullying. It's presumptuous (and stupid) of drama teachers to consider they could have the slightest effect on such an entrenched position by just one effort. Now, mantle of the expert does not presume anything like that. Mantle of the expert work takes time and infinite gradations of perspective, each one chewed over (in different ways) as a deliberately task orientated action. Culture is created so that a trickle of a task becomes a possible Niagara of droplets—and it permits "drudgery bits" and "the most exciting dramatic tension you can imagine" to be in close juxtaposition.

GB: Okay, Dorothy, point taken, if not fully absorbed! Now I know that in this first chapter we have been trying to tease out some of the principles behind mantle of the expert. However, before we move on to look at other examples, could you just give us a flavor of the kind of teacher talk and pupil activities you yourself might have engaged in had *you* been introducing the troubleshooting approach to my second-grade class.

DH: Just a snippet . . .

> Don't you think, if we put our minds to it, we could probably run
> a business that helped other businesses solve problems they
> make for themselves—like forgetting to pay people their wages
> on the right day of the week. . . .

Next stage . . .

> I'm sure we can think of lots of troubles businessmen and
> businesswomen get into through not being careful enough. . .

List making follows, so I discover what "trouble with business" means to this particular class.

Next stage . . . naming our firm.

Next stage . . . developing letterhead and an advertising style.

(None of these need more than blackboard/chalk and talk and then the task of transferring to paper—by the teacher or by the students.)

Next stage . . . testing our advertising out on other teachers, other children, parents, each other, the headteacher, canteen staff, and so forth. This will require some organization because the students will need to be carefully framed so as to preserve their *power to operate* as they actually seek responses to their advertisements. The stages would exactly parallel those in a real-life enterprise:

> One: considering, carefully, in role, our mission statement . . .
> our values . . . the image we wish to convey . . . our style.
> Two: designing, in role, our advertisements . . . taking into
> consideration the target client who will test for us.
> Three: considering, *out* of role, the actual school opportunities
> by which we *in role* may demonstrate our advertising
> models—who would be available to test, and any problems
> (time, numbers) that may arise.
> Four: planning to set up the event so that *the audience*
> understand their part in the proceedings, are prepared to take
> the students' roles seriously (without patronizing!) and are
> prepared to scrutinise and respond to the designs.

Gavin Comments

There seems to be a number of assumptions operating in Dorothy Heathcote's use of mantle of the expert work that stretch the limits of what is normally understood by classroom practice. For instance, both pupils and teacher are contracted to be in some kind of role. This presents a challenge to traditional drama teachers who, although accustomed to engaging in make-believe, may not recognize anything familiar in what Dorothy is offering. A further cause for bewilderment lies in Dorothy's conception of theatre, for implicit in what she is saying so far is a claim that she is working in theatre—with material that seems most untheatrical!

Let me attempt to pin down what are the main features that characterize this mode of education as it has emerged so far in this first chapter. A simple list of what mantle of the expert work requires might be useful:

1. An agreement between teacher and students to take on a
   functional role (i.e., not a character but rather someone
   who is expert in running something).

2. That running takes the form of short-term tasks, always at one remove from actually making a product. The feeling of *caring* about what they are doing and the values they stand for are not simulated, as in some kinds of drama, but are allowed time to accrue naturally.

3. The tasks are normally instigated by the teacher and the students are for most of the time in small groups, which frequently come together to make decisions about policy or corporate action.

4. In order to devise a task, the teacher assesses degree of skill, kind of knowledge and learning area involved, *and* the social health of the class.

5. Each task is seen by the teacher as a carefully selected step in a long series of graded tasks.

6. The chief characteristic of the teacher's role will be that of someone who is dependent on the students' roles for advice and guidance about immediate tasks, but who nevertheless has a strong sense of the firm's past history and of how things used to be done.

7. Above and beyond the specific identifiable skills and other obvious areas of learning, the teacher pursues a continuous goal of raising the students' awareness of how responsibility arising from the particular expertise is part of a value system.

2

Some Introductory Guidelines

■ **We have, in** the first chapter, gone some way toward teasing out principles; in this chapter we start to fill out the method itself, dealing here with ways of beginning.

We have learned so far that the teacher is working, whatever the topic, from the following questions:

What sorts of knowledge/information are to be studied?
What skills (mental, linguistic, artistic, psychomotor, or dramatic) are to be practiced through the knowledge?
What ploys are needed to help special needs of the class?
What will make them reach out and set standards for themselves?

There are four guidelines for the teacher to follow in setting up mantle of the expert.

Presentation

Great care must be taken in presenting the topic effectively: often this is done through teacher talk accompanied by an image in the form of a picture, diagram, map, etc. The *combination* of something to look at and the linguistic style that avoids any instructional note creates entry into the affective framework.

Fiction

The word "if" or the implication of "if" must be introduced early, because there may be such reasonableness in the proposal that some children may think that promises of actual work are being made—

they may think we are *actually* going to run a shoe factory or dig up a burial ground or build a hotel. The teacher must use phrases like,

> Suppose that . . .
> If we could . . .
> If people would let us . . .
> I bet if we tried hard we could . . .

There are many choices of approach—the tone is selected on the basis of what best honors (i.e., takes account of) the attitude or age of the class. For example, a reluctant, turned-off class would possibly do best if the leader indicated in some way that our enterprise has a beat-the-bosses angle. Here the "if" is *implied* by the new tone of voice and posture adopted by the teacher: "You'd think/I think we could do a better job at handling the ambulance driver's strike, wouldn't/don't you?" (Ambulance personnel were on strike in the U.K. at the time we wrote this.) Using "you'd think" permits the remark to be almost thrown away, while "I think" is closer to an assumption that we might be coming a little involved with the business, but not actively—more an invitation to have an opinion. So the teacher's attitude here would suggest "time for bit of a chat," with relevant responses invited.

Moving on: "They never tell us the facts." ("They" implies some vague authority that ought to know better.) "I reckon we could show them a thing or two about an efficient ambulance service."

Of course such talk from the teacher, if students are unused to it, can cause a little confusion, and some teachers are nervous of starting in this way. However, if the visual image (or deflector of attention away from the class to the matter for consideration) is SIGN*ificantly* indicated by placement and form, children very quickly find where they are with it. Remember, all of us, as we enter experiences, try to make sense of what is happening, so we seek to fit unusual events into previously understood or encountered patterns. Students, who spend a large part of their lives making sense of what adults cause to happen, are particularly good at adjusting to events because they are observant sign readers. So when their teacher is showing them something and at the same time talking in a slightly different style, they may wonder, hesitate, and look puzzled but will immediately attempt to readjust. The observant teacher can then reinforce the signs in the very next statement. The teacher's own sense of her body image, the position she selects in relation to the class and the object, will all be part of this signing system, which forms the *process* of teaching.

What such teacher talk is doing is slightly "raising the curtain," inviting the class to take a peep at the metaphorical stage where fiction can take place. When the teacher says, "I reckon we could show them . . .," who is *we*? *Who* is she addressing? She is obviously not talking as a teacher to a class; she is giving a *hint* of the roles they will all be playing when the curtain goes up completely. Of course she could more straightforwardly have explained in a "teacher" way (as Gavin did with bullying): "Would you like to do a drama about helping to bring the ambulance strike to an end?"

Dynamic of Action

The frame of *power to operate* must be laid in very directly and clearly. For example, let us assume that our class of students has shown great interest in the ambulance personnel's strike and that we can see its relevance to the curriculum, then we may choose to establish them in role as members of the ACAS (Advisory, Conciliation and Arbitration Service), a body in the U.K. that deals with industrial impasse. (The U.S. counterpart is the National Labor Relations Board.)

Of course most drama teachers doing a drama about a strike would immediately cast the students as ambulance personnel and bosses and go for a dramatic conflict! Mantle of the expert does not work this way; it works obliquely—learning about one thing by looking through something else. In this case the students will learn about ambulance workers by looking through the process of mediation.

The first presentation and the first tasks must therefore establish the function of mediators. It is not necessary to label *us* at this point; we don't have to be called ACAS mediators; the name is less important than the *power to function*. As we shall see in the examples later in the book, initially the teacher does not have to *call* the class monks or scientists. But the major task, or power to operate, is clearly stated: "We've got letters from both sides now . . . asking for a meeting . . . separately, of course."

A Past History and an Implied Future

"We've got letters from both sides" raises the curtain fully, for now we want our students to respond as characters do at the beginning of a play—with an implied history. An *in situ* context with a past and a future must be established. This means that the children and teacher enter their expert business in the middle, as it were. This follows a basic theatre law: characters are engaged in an event when they and the audience meet in the play; Hamlet's father's ghost has appeared upon the battlements of Elsinore often enough in the past for the soldiers to have told Horatio, who in turn has summoned Hamlet to participate in the oft-repeated haunting. Thus the present time summons the past and presages the future.

But of course our students are not to be characters in the psychological sense that a playwright and an audience would expect, but rather as a *collective,* CHARACTER*izing expertise,* a group of people committed to a worldview of responsibility. They will grow into this responsibility and expertise gradually over a period of time, just like an actor slowly builds a character through rehearsal time. In Gavin's bullying session, the students' ownership of their role as responsible advisers to schools was no more than an actor's surface adoption of a role at a first rehearsal.

We have called the above "guidelines" rather than "steps" because they are not meant to suggest a particular order of doing things. Indeed it is likely that guideline 3, the dynamic of action, will dictate how the other guidelines should be followed. Having a grasp of 3, the teacher then works backward in planning to reach a suitable starting point for the particular class, based, as we have already said, on the skills and attitudes of the pupils.

Let us look in some detail at how planning might be affected. The teacher knows she is going to find herself saying, "We've got letters from both sides now . . . asking for a meeting . . . separately, of course." In the lesson plan, therefore, she has to decide what nondrama activities the class should engage in as preparation for responding to that particular teacher approach.

Such an activity might be "thinking of what we know about ambulance people's responsibilities" or "listing all the things we think ambulance workers do in a typical day" or "drawing a plan of the inside of an ambulance."

Working backward in planning has its hazards, of course, for the planner is choosing from a number of possible backward routes. Making this selection requires a firm grip on criteria. At first sight the above examples of possible early steps seem appropriate, and indeed they would help the children feel their way into the problem. But would such exercises meet the requirements of guideline 4, building a past and a future? They would certainly contribute to building the concept of the *ambulance employees'* past and future, but it is the past and future of the *experts* that needs to be established—and in this case, the teacher has decided that the experts are to be the mediators, not the ambulance people. The *logic* has to be right. So if she feels it is necessary to reinforce the students' knowledge of ambulance workers in this way, she does so knowing that although the class will feel that the work has started, it is in fact temporarily off target. Making a list of all the kinds of arbitration problems (e.g., arguments arising from changing shifts or work patterns, promotion rivalries, rules about discipline, new training requirements) might be an equivalent start that takes the students more directly into their mediation roles.

When the teacher does eventually reach "We've got letters from both sides now . . . asking for a meeting . . separately, of course," how are the students to see the implications behind this and where does she go from there? As the teacher says this, there must be visible evidence of letters around or in her hands, with authentic-seeming letterhead, content, signatures, etc. The word "now" is the present, summoning the past, and the words "separately, of course" presage future action that the next sign must immediately initiate. For example, "Are any of you using the arbitration suite on the third floor this morning?" permits the slightest response (either yes or no) and it does not matter at all if some say one thing and some another. There is no need to be afraid of confusion.

If the suite on the third floor seems to be in use, everyone just needs to agree on "how many suites we *might* have available in ACAS headquarters if we were going to help sort the ambulance workers' disagreement." At this point it might be useful to agree on the design of our building (an activity, it will now be seen, to more purpose than designing ambulances) *and* all the different disputes we are currently mediating. Thus our past and present work comes into high focus. Some students will enjoy the game of inventing disputes (which will enter the ACAS archives—nothing can be irresponsibly thrown in), but some teachers may prefer to arm themselves in advance with ongoing disputation work: "Which group is arbitrating the salmonella/microwave oven manufacturers scare? Who's dealing with the meeting of the British Medical Association representatives and the Junior Minister of Health? How far are we with that libel case about . . .?" Students will easily hook themselves into such intractable cases because they sense the power to operate such problems bring to them in the context of the ACAS.

If such a pattern emerges, then something must occur that overtly causes everyone to recognize that "we are working in the ACAS."

This occurrence must be a *task:* making our entry permits or our name tags, filling in a form to requisition a room under the heading of the case one of the groups is dealing with. Thus, the expertise is now established and all can undertake these early commitment tasks outside the role work. Discussions on how badges, name tags, permits, room requisition forms, should look will take place and formats will be established and things will get made. During such times the teacher will be moving linguistically between the role-time "now" ("A lot of people have commented on how helpful it is to be able to see our names as soon as they arrive") and task-oriented talk such as "These forms will have to look very professional, so let's get them really well cut and fixed."

Teacher-in-role is a feature of much classroom drama, but a mantle of the expert approach demands a particularly mercurial version(!), with the teacher frequently engaged in hopping deftly, sliding elliptically, switching abruptly, or even bestriding the two worlds of fiction and reality. It may be just a matter of *seconds* that a role is held and then dropped—and then assumed again. It is even possible to convey with a word and the raising of an eyebrow a deliberate ambiguity between the two. It is also something of a paradox that the *in-role* usage breeds a healthy teacher/student relationship, whereas *out-of-role* talk and actions foreshadow the adventure and power of the drama. Both are essential.

To summarize: there are four guidelines for the teacher to follow in planning a mantle of the expert approach:

1. Present the area of expertise effectively using a combination of teacher talk and visual image.
2. Introduce 'if' early on, and in a way that will appeal to the particular class. (Give the students a glimpse through the partially raised curtain!)
3. Give the group power to *function*. This gives the work its overall dynamic in respect of what is seen as the major task, but many other minor steps may have to be taken by the class before this dynamic is harnessed.
4. Build a past, present and future. (The curtain goes up!)

The Dimension Factor: Using the Mantle of the Expert Approach Across the Curriculum

■ **Although a curriculum** is likely to be made up of separate subjects, the recognition of its personal, social, societal, and epistemological aspects will give a sense of coherence and overall purpose to discrete learning areas. In the British National Curriculum these cross-curricular features are referred to as "dimension."

A unique feature of the mantle of the expert approach to education is that this dimension, this looking at a part of a subject in terms of the whole, is built into the heart of the method. Any one subject or learning area is both interconnected with a broad spectrum of knowledge and, more important, *understood by the learner* to be so connected.

This dimension may be clearly identified and emphasized in state and national curriculum documents, but that does not guarantee that cross-curricular referencing by the teacher and student will occur. Indeed, traditional methods of teaching militate *against* the possibility of this happening. The division of the curriculum into separate subject areas encourages learners to conceive of distinct pockets of knowledge. Some schools and teacher-education institutions are aware of the danger and seek to overcome the problem, at least with kindergarten and elementary classes, by introducing "projects" or "topics." Typically, student teachers would be expected to be capable of devising a central project for their class so rich in its elements that all the subjects of the curriculum would be covered while the total experience preserved both continuity and coherence.

On the surface, this appears entirely satisfactory. The students are given a project—on weather, for example—that takes them into geography, mathematics, science, language arts, literature, and even music—a total experience of weather, or so it is claimed. But the wide variety of weather activities do not necessarily offer a *dimension of wholeness*. What is finally impressed on the students may be a sense of how many *different* aspects of weather there are.

Knowledge Is Experienced by a Responsible Human Being

The problem with dividing a topic into its constituent parts is that it is, *and remains,* a necessarily intellectual process of categorizing. There is no *center* to the knowledge. There is only a title and its many subdivisions. Mantle of the expert provides a *center* for all knowledge: it is always experienced by the students in terms of the responsible human being. Thus, interconnectedness between one aspect and the whole is *unquestionable.* There is a sense in which an aspect *is* the whole and vice versa.

THE RESPONSIBLE HUMAN BEING MUST BE A SERVICER, NOT A RECEIVER

Participants in mantle of the expert are *framed* as servicers committed to an enterprise. This frame fundamentally affects their relationship with knowledge. They can never be mere receivers "told" about knowledge. They can only engage with it as people with a *responsibility.* This responsibility is not to knowledge itself, although, paradoxically, that is what the students are indirectly acquiring, but to the enterprise they have undertaken. Knowledge becomes information, evidence, source material, specification, records, guidelines, regulations, theories, formulas, and artifacts, all of which are *to be interrogated.* This is an *active, urgent, purposeful* view of learning, in which knowledge is to be *operated on,* not merely to be taken in.

The teacher must plan for a continuing investigative relationship between the student and the information to be researched. There is a clear pattern to this planning, prompted by a series of questions. Take the following example, in which the mantle of the expert context is cattle farming:

Questions

1. To what end do the students require the information?

2. From what frame of reference should the interrogation of the information take place?

3. How will the information be shaped and placed when they first meet it?

Answers

1. The information is to be in the area of genetics with a class of twelve-year-olds.

2. Students are framed as agricultural technicians engaged in a research project for Indian farmers.

3. The information is presented in the form of an English farmer's records of building up a herd of purebred holstein cattle over a period of thirty years with all the genetic information correctly recorded, plus notes on feed and milk yields. The records are on computer and in a written form made to be easily accessible to beginners, especially regarding the genetic information. For example, all cows and bulls have names and numbers that enable easy tracing backward and forward through the gene bank.

4. What tasks or series of tasks will engage the students in interrogating the information?

4. The research project frame demands that agricultural personnel use the existing genetic information to work out, and illustrate as they try to do so, how normal holstein cattle, which are always black and white, can, by judicious genetic breeding, be reduced in size and bred to be all white in color in order to survive on the small acreage of many Indian farms. (This is a real issue—there are farms in India where very small white cattle can feed under low growing trees on crops grown specially for fodder.) The necessary information is all in the records. The precise task of changing size and predicting color is the interrogatory stance. The recording process is on a large sheet of paper (or on a blackboard), using the correct "genetic script" of the farmer's records.

5. Which tools are required by the task?

5. The tools are the genetic records, the public writing materials, including colored pens for tracing genetic patterns through the generations. *And* the science teacher, who is in role as the farmer, must not be too quick at checking her own records. This "slowness" is part of the enabling process that has replaced merely telling.

6. What form will be used to preserve the knowledge gained so that it can be applied at future times?

6. The information will finally be contained in a *Farmer's Weekly* article. Farmers will be encouraged to participate in the scheme over the next five years.

THE RESPONSIBLE HUMAN BEING IN THE STUDENT REACHES BEYOND PRESENT CAPABILITIES

A readiness theory of learning (derived from Piaget and others) sets a false limit on a student's capacity. It ignores the Vygotskian observations on socially determined learning contexts: that in the presence of an empowering adult a child can reach beyond his own capacity in carrying out a task. Teacher-in-role enhances this particular adult function. The teacher, through her role, provides a model of high expectations for the enterprise that at first seems out of reach, but that, in time, the student seeks to emulate: framed as a human being responsible for the enterprise, he has no choice but to aim beyond his normal ability—and to break the confines of rigidly held concepts. Here are two examples of young children's lateral thinking:

1. Six-year-old rose growers had to help the 1920s ace flyer, Amy Johnson, get her tiny plane out of their rose garden, where she had landed when short of fuel. They advised her "never to fly above the blue" because she wouldn't be able to "ever come back." When she asked why, they thought it was "something to do with the shape of the plane and the world."

2. Nine-year-old children working in role as students of medical history explained to a "portrait" of Dr. Lister that his contribution to medicine in the nineteenth century was that by using carbolic he paved the way for modern doctors to have Band-Aids, and that his rigid stethoscope would in future be used by car mechanics to listen to "heartbeats" of internal combustion engines as well as those of babies still in their mothers' tummies.

THE RESPONSIBLE HUMAN BEING SEES A ROAD AHEAD

From the very first task the student has a sense of "going somewhere." At first a mantle of the expert approach will develop on the narrowest of roads, following a thin, fog-enveloped footpath that seems to finish with the end of the task—much work in schools can be like this—but successful completion of the first task invites the student to look at where he has just walked and to look for the next path, a little wider and lighter, seeing more of where he is going. And as he learns to share the ever-widening road with others, seeing the tasks as stewardship of their enterprise, he gains a conception of a complex landscape. This is the *dimension,* critical to mantle of the expert, that is so often missing for the traditionally taught student.

Student Teacher Takes On the Topic Approach

Armed with the theoretical conviction that children need to be engaged in cooperative work that involves them in wide varieties and levels of tasks and the notion of a teacher as a supporting helper, our anonymous aspirant prepares a classroom project based on a model still found in pedagogic publications. Teachers find it useful and *comforting,* as it seems to offer a secure starting point, sound and dependable. Our student teacher chooses *China* as the topic—it is almost Chinese New Year—and maps out subtopics as shown in Figure 3-1. This clustered grouping delineates the possibility of learning about China through a large variety of interesting aspects, which seem interrelated. The shape on the page, which is indicative of her thinking, as yet provides no intimations of cross-curricular work, but no doubt she intends that to occur. This layout will guide her in collecting material. The marvelous proliferation of resources will involve a lot of sifting and then selecting or rejecting as suitable or unsuitable "for the age of her class"—a safe criterion for the traditional teacher. She will probably collect Chinese myths, pictures of dragons, maps, paintings, modern Chinese artifacts, statistics, and recipes; there will be authentic music, rice bowls, chopsticks, even "moon cakes" since it is close to the Chinese New Year.

Having assembled a mouth-watering collection, her next problem is how to start the topic. Probably she'll clear her classroom walls, ready to refill them with the impressive China work she and her students will be producing: a map of China with principal towns and regions marked; a celestial five-toed dragon; recipes; a take-out menu from a Chinese restaurant, with Chinese characters alongside the English translation; drawings of the Great Wall; Chinese stories; and pictures of modern China.

The tasks for the students will probably take the form of a lively discussion and research about where China is and what they know about it. Their ideas will be recorded in some way, each child perhaps making a personal contribution to the class "book about China." They

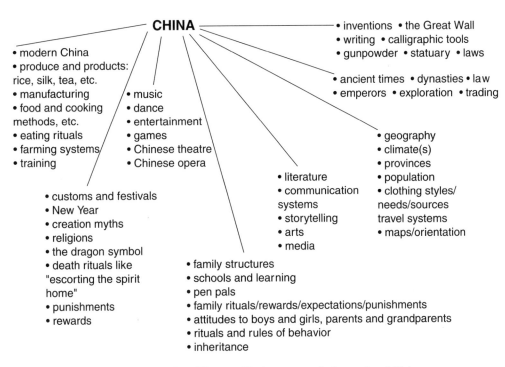

FIGURE 3-1. *A Student Teacher Plans a Project around the topic of* China.

may look in atlases to locate places to put on the "big map." The teacher will note the skills the students are practicing in these research processes. She will try to follow their interest and supplement their knowledge or direct them to further research into the school library resources on China. She will respond with whatever seems to keep everyone actively engaged in the work, while at the same time trying to ensure that different aspects of the curriculum are covered.

A Teacher Takes a Mantle of the Expert Approach to the Topic

To get a clearer picture of the mantle of the expert methodology, let's look at a teacher as she applies it to this same topic, *China*. She first asks herself a number of questions:

1. What kind of people *need to know* about China?

   - Media reporters
   - Travel agents
   - Missionaries

- Trade missions
- Medical people
- Entrepreneurs setting up businesses or factories
- United Nations staff
- Ambassadorial staff
- Historians
- TV producers or filmmakers

2. Which different domains of concern will be activated by work undertaken by the above kinds of people because of their primary and secondary duties?
3. How can records (legitimate to the enterprise) be kept of information as it emerges, so that the information can be used again?
4. How can information be presented with a minimum of "telling"?

To help her answer questions 2–4, our teacher examines the list of people who *need* to know about China and amplifies it into categories:

1. *Service enterprises where no goods are produced,* where all the tasks are in support of other people: a bank, a hotel, a library, a restaurant, a hospital, a travel agency, a veterinary clinic, a store, a fire station.
2. *Manufacturing enterprises, which make things:* a shoe factory, a dairy, a bakery, a flour mill, a brewery, a fashion house, a steel works, a publishing house, a commercial herb garden.
3. *Charitable or administrative enterprises:* OXFAM (the famine relief organization), the National Trust or the English Heritage (organizations that preserve England's great houses and historical sites), the Salvation Army, Greenpeace.
4. *Nurturing enterprises:* homes for orphaned or unwanted children, hospices for the sick and dying, play groups, a gene bank for animals and plants, a national park, a nature reserve, a social service agency.
5. *Regulatory enterprises:* police stations; customs, tax, and immigration bureaus; prisons; justice departments; the armed services.
6. *Skilled artisans, who maintain things:* plumbers, electricians, stonemasons, joiners, repairers of antique furniture, archivists.

7. *Arts enterprises:* a theatre, a photographic studio, an art gallery, a craft center, an opera or ballet company.
8. *Establishments dedicated to helping people learn:* sports training centers, museums, zoos.

Many of these, at least at first glance, seem irrelevant to China, but sometimes a closer look bears fruit in unexpected ways. The categorization step is important because the purpose of an enterprise to a certain extent influences the mind set and frames any mission statement.

TRAVEL AGENCY

After looking at her categorized list, our teacher decides that a *travel agency* seems suited to the study of a foreign country. Now, a travel agency would certainly take the students into those aspects of China that were in the student teacher's plan: modern China, the Great Wall, food and cooking, customs, would all have to be considered when arranging tours and tickets. Also it would be easy to envisage the clients. Using the convention of written orders from clients specifying dates, tickets, etc., would generate tasks for the class. One can imagine the students poring over detailed maps of China, planning journeys to make connections with ferries, trains, and buses, and explaining in leaflets to customers what was available for the eager tourist.

There is, however, one snag! Travel agents deal with distances, timetables, and the twenty-four-hour clock. They do *not* examine stories or history textbooks in order to advise their clients, so it would not be reasonable for them to do the kind of research the teacher requires—in other words, travel agents do not *need to know.*

A TRADE DELEGATION

Therefore our mantle of the expert teacher scans the categories again to see whether there is a more useful idea. How about a trade delegation testing out the possibilities of starting a car-manufacturing enterprise in China? (Volkswagen has indeed just begun such an enterprise.) This demands straight research from the delegation workers:

1. Where are the towns where goods can be transported in and out?
2. What transport systems are available for the many materials to be delivered?
3. What supply industries are available? steel mills? power plants? Is there an available work force?

4. Will people moving to China to start the enterprise have to adapt to the housing styles and schooling system?
5. How will cultural matters—religious practices, family life, working hours, work hierarchies, work ethic, modes of address—affect the enterprise?
6. What is the attitude of the Chinese to our country and outsiders in general regarding trade?

All these seem to confirm the idea of a trade delegation, so the teacher begins to organize these tasks? What images arise from the above list of what the students will be doing? *Maps* will matter in relation to 1 and 2 above. They need to be detailed and up to date, so the textbook type of map is inefficient. One map will supply information on *placement*—rivers, railways, roads, airports, seaports, cities and towns. A second map will be specialized, giving mineral information and showing places where these have traditionally been exploited. So far the idea holds, but how will mantle of the expert be different from students just looking at maps for information, as in the traditional method? First, the maps will not be the first resource used, and when they are used the mental set of the workers will reflect focused, precise inquiries that (possibly urgently) require answers at the speed of phone calls rather than leisurely note taking.

Now, how to find a precise starting point? No one *forces* a business enterprise to work in China, so a circumstance must be invented that will reasonably prompt a firm to want to work overseas. This is the central question and at this point the car industry seems *un*suitable to our teacher, since it is related to *profits* and the *cheapness* of labor. So what could a purpose be other than merely profit? An *invitation* from the Chinese government to open up a computerized car factory? An invitation would certainly widen the purpose, and the experts would find it reasonable to be asked to use their knowledge in the service of another country. Considering another country could allow us to perceive cars and their purposes in a new light—perhaps to develop a car suitable to the special life and culture of that country? Perhaps an electric car based on the rickshaw principle? It would certainly lessen the hardships of a great many people. But the students must not patronize the Chinese culture and their way of doing things. This frame would enable the experts to study the living arrangements of the rural Chinese; it would include transport, work traditions, locations, food, and farming. Also cars and rickshaws have a logical connection. That's more like it! And the *electric* rickshaw idea could be extended to designing ambulances for difficult terrain, which would tie in with China's history of caring for and treating the sick.

Check the pattern now: The *government* has the power to *invite* experts to *design something important to its people,* which *develops from something* already in the Chinese culture. Therefore, this frame does not patronise—*it is a partnership.*

There is a problem here, however. Experts making vehicles would study what was necessary to build efficient machines, build them, and then *leave*—they would not necessarily be interested in a deep study of China! So long as they researched roads, the territory, the loads to be carried, they could remain isolated (and insulated!) from China as a culture with a history. It's a pity to have to abandon the car-manufacturing idea, but mantle of the expert must have integrity.

So what about running a hotel in order to train Chinese staff regarding the expectations of Western tourists? This happens in African countries where accommodation must be close to safari and game parks. The *park* gives rise to the *need* of accommodation, which in turn demands *people* to service the hotel in all aspects. But how can this be adapted to the China topic? Who would the experts be? They can't be Chinese, because they have grown up in another country. This *is* a coil. Somehow the experts from the Western world must find themselves needing to learn about Chinese culture in order to advise the Chinese about Western expectations. The problem is how to represent the Chinese staff who would be running the hotel?

Suddenly there is a solution! The students have to research Chinese culture as hotel experts who specialize in training staffs in those parts of the world people wish to visit because they *are* so special—because of their art, history, cultural sites, rare animals, inventions, museums, and rituals. Because we train people, we can invent the kind of location a Hollywood film might require—absolutely authentic, based on our research. This mantle of the expert would not require any Chinese staff because it would set up a "test project." Try out this pattern:

- Western *hotel experts* who understand the needs and attitudes of Western clients *respond to a request* from the Chinese Tourist Association to *build a "training school" hotel* (*not* a real hotel).
- The experts first have to *research Chinese culture* so as to outfit the hotel in the proper style, reflecting Chinese foods, decor, traditions, etc.
- Then they have to *prepare the courses of instruction very carefully,* so that the Chinese tourist board can run the "hotel" and train staff members to anticipate Western tourists. This could involve making videos, preparing

phrase books, designing Chinese menus that encourage Western guests to try the food.

The training angle allows the "experts" to study China in order to provide an authentic background for both clients (who *expect* a Chinese hotel) and staff members (who work in Chinese hotels)! Having done this they then have to examine *their* cultural expectations in order to plan the training course to enable Chinese staff members to help Western tourists feel comfortable and safe while enjoying, respecting and penetrating the culture they've come to explore. Whew!

This uncertainty in the planning stage of mantle of the expert is typical and can feel very worrisome, much more so than the apparently straightforward pattern of the model developed by our traditional student teacher. But, as you've seen, the result is far superior.

Part Two

From Exploration to Presentation

Life in a Mediaeval Monastery

■ **The piece of work** discussed in this chapter is an elaboration of a plan carried out by Dorothy Heathcote with a student teacher who was about to begin three weeks of practice teaching. We will attempt to flesh out the original plan in a way that goes beyond a description of "steps to be taken in the lesson."

First, along with a possible set of planning procedures, we elaborate on special points in the way a tutor might do in a lecture or seminar, exploring with the students the reasons and implications behind a particular ploy. We discuss the ideal goals and achievements and consider alternatives for adapting the work to a particular classroom. Next, we discuss the "Bishop's letter" device in detail and then conclude with a brief record of what actually happened in the student teacher's classroom. We hope that you will find this juxtaposition of the "ideal" and the "pragmatic" useful.

Establishing the Context

The student teacher wanted the class, in a Church of England primary school, to understand something of the lifestyle of monks living in a monastery in the Middle Ages. As the school was in Durham, which has its own cathedral (formerly a monastery), the topic seemed particularly appropriate. She was interested in trying out a mantle of the expert approach, which would involve the students in "running" a monastery. She also wanted to include *all* the curriculum subjects, with a special emphasis on *science.* She eventually decided to exclude math from the exercise, while realizing that it *could* have been included as part of the mantle of the expert approach.

She discussed with Dorothy what should give the whole work its *dynamic.* She decided that *creating a book of monastery rules* would allow a process of realizing what they had learned and would provide entry to the science curriculum if the book was made from *handmade paper.* To sum up: adopting the work of monks would stimulate the children to find out about monasteries; and the book of rules would be a way of reinforcing what they had learned, would involve significant art, language, and science work, and would finally be evidence for the student teacher that something had been learned. The task itself might be undertaken in many classrooms, but in this particular case it will be done in the "as if" mode of drama: instead of the usual implicit purpose behind any children's activity—it is the teacher's idea of "a good educational thing to be doing"—a dramatic context provides the *raison d'être.*

At some early stage of the work, the students, working in role as monks, receive a letter from Bishop Anselm (see Appendix A) requesting a book of rules to assist a house of nuns his sister wishes to form in Chichester. This provides the momentum for the rest of the work. (See Guideline in Chapter 2). This chapter suggests stages of work up to the point of opening this letter.

It is characteristic of the mantle of the expert approach that it involves pupils in classroom tasks—reading, sorting information, writing, arts and crafts, science, math, and so on—just the kinds of activity they are typically invited to engage in by all teachers everywhere. The argument put forward in this book is that because the students are to be in role in a fictional context, they will bring a sense of responsibility to their learning, with the result that the teacher is able, through the drama, to make greater demands on the students than if this alternative trigger to learning were missing.

To keep it simple in setting out possible procedures we will address you, the reader, as though we are giving *you* advice, as though *you* are inexperienced. Occasionally, at relevant points of the plan, we will include illustrations. For the description of the initial steps the right-hand pages list the strategies to be employed and the left-hand pages provide comments and theoretical elaboration. (These points are lettered consecutively for easy cross-reference.)

Please remember that although the following *looks like* a carefully refined plan—and there are certainly aspects of it that could contribute to such a plan—it is intended to give the *flavor* of a variety of possible approaches. In the same way, examples of the kinds of things the teacher might say in and out of role (set in italics) are also meant only to give a flavor; they are not there to be learned parrot-fashion.

Incorporating the work into the school day is also meant to be very flexible—from the entire day to a brief session every day to anything in between. In the early stages described in this chapter, it is envisioned that the students are engaged in other "normal" school work, picking up the monastery work occasionally. Once the monastery work becomes established, incorporating most of the curriculum subjects, then it would ideally be appropriate for it to take up most of the school day.

Possible Strategies

A. Show pictures of a monastery or cathedral.

B. Hand out twenty cards, each bearing the name of a monastery job such as cellarer, abbot, herbalist, almoner. *"These are some people who ran a cathedral or a monastery. Can you guess what they did . . . what they were in charge of? They're funny words, some of them. Shall I put our guesses on the blackboard?"*

C. Now give out the answers, carefully handwritten on another set of cards. Each card describes one job or duty. For example: I LOOK AFTER ALL THE LINEN WE USE AT MEALTIMES AND IN OUR CHURCH. THE CLOTHS FOR THE ALTAR ARE VERY SPECIAL. Invite the class to gather around a big table and try to match the two sets of cards, trying to fit the label with the description, referring, of course, to their guesses on the blackboard and amending them as they come to new conclusions.

D. Read out the "right" answers, asking the class to rearrange the cards as necessary.

E. Making a fresh start, give out the work description cards again, one to each child *and* to yourself.

1. Each student is to read out what it says on his or her card—you may care to read yours out first.

Comments

A. If you are lucky enough to be living in a European city that has preserved its cathedral, you will no doubt take your students through it. This student teacher lived in Durham, England, where there is an impressive cathedral.

B. Some teachers worry that the students find the names too difficult to read. Please take a risk—children enjoy guessing, and don't forget that mantle of the expert tends to invite the youngest children to take bigger strides than usual!

C. Notice that the card descriptions have slipped into the *personal: I* look after the linen. . . . So it's no longer what *they,* some historical figures in the past do, but what *I* do. As the students chat to each other about how the cards should be matched, you will make encouraging (not *correcting*) comments: *"Mmm . . . yes . . . you would think almoner has to do with almonds."* This also introduces young children to the idea that it is safe to be wrong, that guessing and getting incorrect answers is a *normal* classroom procedure; it is not a *mistake* as such.

D. Because *you* know that this preliminary task has been a first step toward moving into a fictional context (which in this case would require them to live and behave as monks), "reading the answers" is an opportunity to move imperceptibly into the here and now of "being there," *as if* the abbot, not the teacher, is reading the duties to the brethren. This *hint* of moving into the dramatic present is a device to which we shall constantly refer. Its power lies in its ambivalence. It is not *explained* to the class that teacher is now going to address them as if. No, it must *dawn* on the pupils from teacher's subtle change of voice, change of posture, change from teacher smile to reader/abbot seriousness that something is going on. You can pick up the paper with the list of answers and deliberately slip it inside an old-looking (burlap bound?) book, as if it is the book that is being read from. Thus you will be indicating two things at once: (1) this is not real, I am playing a game and (2) this *is* real. It is as an outcome of this sense of things being dramatic that the pupils then proceed to "correct" the positions of some of the cards. On the other hand, you may prefer simply to explain, *"I'm going to read these out, as though we are those monks."*

E.

1.

2. *"Shut your eyes. See if you can see what happens when the work mentioned on the card is being done."*

3. *"In a minute, I'm going to ask you to tell your neighbor what you saw happening when you shut your eyes. I'll show you what I mean. I'll tell my neighbor here* [the nearest student] *what I saw my person doing—I've got the abbot.* [To your neighbor] *I see him walking at the back of a procession of monks as they go into the chapel for Mass. When they kneel in their places he goes to the high altar. I notice* [your hand touching the book, perhaps] *the prayer book is already at the right page. I shall read its Latin text."*

4. *"Close your eyes again and see how much detail of what happens you can notice. Open your eyes—and tell your neighbor."*

5. Each student (or a selection of volunteers) can now tell the whole class what he or she has heard; corrections or questions are now in order.

6. You explain to the class that now that we have heard all the duties, we need time to think which one each student would like to choose "for keeps." Suggest a group of students mount the cards on the classroom wall so that they hang there to be pondered on until we resume our work on monasteries—perhaps not until the next school day. Tell them *you* will keep the abbot card.

F. A group of students mount the cards at some free time during the day.

G. Another fresh start: you now introduce the class to the plan of the monastery (Appendix B). Which you will have prepared on a large piece of paper. You will gather them round and invite their comments about what the different rooms are and the kind of duties that are likely to go on in each.

H. A critical moment of choice: invite your class to choose their roles. There are a number of ways of doing this. One would be to invite each student in turn to stand by the sheet of mounted duties

2. Notice the word "happens"—it invites discover of *how* each sees.

3. This strategy of using yourself as a model gives students permission to observe detail, thus setting a standard. You deliberately slip from "he" to "I," anticipating some of the students might do likewise.

4. As they talk to each other, listen for which students saw *themselves* carrying out the duty and which saw someone else.
5.

6.

F.

G. Although the ostensible purpose for introducing the monastery plan here is to enable the students to make choices about which kinds of responsibility they want to take on in their role as monks, you will of course have the whole curriculum at the back of your mind and, in particular, the fictitious letter from the bishop (Appendix A) that will lead into the science and math work. Therefore, while listening to their comments you will drop in questions and musings that will plant concepts for future reference. Thus you will gently reinforce any of their comments relating to *size* of a particular room or the *number* of people that it would comfortably hold. For example the opportunity might arise (in passing!) to muse upon the number of beds the refectory might hold. Thus you are opening up the dimension of *size* as just one of many ways of considering a plan. You do this knowing that a central feature of their future work is to respond to the bishop's request for an expansion of the Scriptorium and that seeing a plan in terms of bodies in spaces will be a critical skill.
H. Your preference may be to instruct: *"Let's have four people for each role."* However, if you adopt the former method, then you will find yourself saying *with no emphasis* that at this time *"we have no*

and point to or read out the one chosen. A grouping will emerge as others follow, some roles being more popular than others.

I. One straightforward way of getting them to try out their newly acquired roles would be to give a "teacher" kind of instruction: *"Spread yourselves round the classroom and try miming the kind of tasks you think your role would be responsible for each day."* We would recommend, however, that where possible you give the above instruction *through the drama,* using your role as abbot to do so.

You do it through abbot-style language and through a simple communal action of breaking and sharing a loaf of bread: *"Brothers* [a simple vocal shift, a change of stance (hands in metaphoric sleeves), a pen (thick, brown) taken up] *before we depart today to our daily work in this place dedicated to the glory of Jesus and all his works* [moving to the large table already prepared with large sheet of brown paper—('public size,' as Dorothy calls it)] *let us break bread together* [swiftly drawing a loaf of bread, either modern sliced or the seemingly less anachronistic dry-oven-baked loaf on the sheet, and drawing in the 'breaks,' enough for all—see Figure 4-1]."

Then use *both hands* to give "from" the drawing (the "paper sign") to each individual child with portentous energy and pace a "piece of bread." (If the loaf is sliced, the hands must shape the delicate thin-

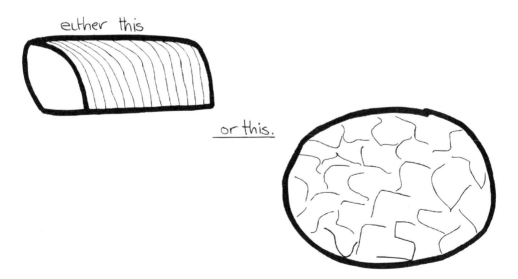

FIGURE 4-1. *Bread Drawings.*

• •

cellarer" [note the we—accepting and sharing the implications of their choices]. *"Perhaps later some of the brothers will help us undertake such duties."* Or pressing harder, *"We have no experienced bread makers. We will have to bake our bread as best we can."*

I. Notice the suggested language here. Whereas before you were ambiguously hinting at being in role when you read the duties, now, once the pupils have committed themselves, you firmly use the dramatic present, respecting their role functions and reinforcing the feeling that it is happening in the here and now—again a diagnostic moment, for you will at the same time be testing how individual pupils appear to be responding to this new "game" by the way they respond to the abbot: degree of embarrassment? extent of self-protection? need to undermine the game? appropriateness or inappropriateness of language style, particularly whether they are able to use "I am" rather than "They would"? dependence on the natural class leader for the go-ahead?

Now you are to give the children the experience of you and them working as monks together, through the frame of a ritual. This has to be done with some accomplishment. It is worth looking in detail at the following carefully built structure:

1. Now the drama action is going to begin
2. Now I shall become the abbot
3. Thus endowing you with "brotherness"
4. Creating a religious order
5. Initiating our common understanding of Christianity
6. Creating our first ceremony
7. And sending you out to your personal work.

The above messages are among those you will need to signal within the first few moments as you accomplish this first real dramatizing; and you will need to recognize that it will require you to use your voice, your vocabulary, your stance as abbot, the way you occupy space, the way you handle or mime objects to symbolize a ceremony, and your general demeanour *with a subtlety that is both theatrical and reassuring,* so that your students feel they are part of the theatre that is being created. This is likely to be but a fleeting few moments of shared theatre, for when they disperse into their "working monks" groups, it will simply be their role *functions,* not their sense of form and order that will take over.

(Note: the line highlighted with asterisks demands the shift from friendly teacher to benign Abbot.)

ness; if a cob, strong fingers tear into its heavier crustiness.) Please do not see yourself as the *character* of the abbot—you are *their teacher* demonstrating the kind of gesture that by tacit agreement signs abbot to all present, including yourself!

Then, holding *your* piece, eating slowly, savoring, pacing the ceremony, pronounce, *"The hand of our Lord was upon this morning's bakehouse labors."*

Finally, fold the drawing with a *teacher's* smile and place the pen and folded paper aside: *"Shall we begin our monk's work now? *I shall be in the scriptorium if I am needed—you only have to seek me out."**

J. Come out of role; invite the students to comment on what the abbot did: *"Did it seem okay to talk like that? What about the breaking of the bread—was my 'signing' clear enough? Does anyone know what 'drama eyes' are?"*

Move the discussion to what would be a typical task carried out as part of each monk's duties—think back to the images they described to each other earlier. In their newly chosen groups (composed of students who have chosen the same card), ask them to help each other make a still picture or tableau showing each individual monk doing a particular, repetitive job. *"Get your group to check that everyone can read what you are working at, what tools you are using."*

K. The above exercise (J) will only last a few minutes, as the students are unlikely to have the knowledge or the skill to sustain anything but superficial meaning. However, your comments will be feeding them the idea of getting at the truth through *detail.* You may

· ·

J. This establishes the regular need to "read for meaning," using yourself, on this occasion, as a model. The conscious explanation of their "drama eyes" permits them to expand and contract the dimensions of the actual classroom space at will. Walls dissolve into vistas, ceilings into sky, and floors into pits of darkness by *conscious will.* At these times they share with artists the mind expansion that is essential not only to their safety in the fictional dimensions of the work, but to the sustenance of those invented worlds. The emphasis is not on shutting out intrusive reality, but on conjuring the necessary images to fill the mind and yet remain in charge of images made.

You can reawaken and support the "inner spectator" by moving among the still figures commenting on what you see—no guesses!—only what you *see.* Neither must any value judgment be made or motive surmised. For example, a sweeping monk cannot have a real brush, so the teacher cannot discuss brushes. This kind of comment is possible: *"I see here one who is intent upon some action regarding the floor; he stands poised and with energy; his eyes are firmly watching what is in his hands as his hands firmly guide it."* These statements will always be positive, and be heard clearly by others; no child will be taken by surprise—you will move deliberately, delicately as regards space. Very precisely, by positioning, let everyone realize who is being commented on. No lies can be told, no quality mentioned that the person will recognize as untrue, because this immediately creates pretense as well as moves the "spectator" in the child away from self-monitoring to considering teacher, who must, wherever possible function almost as Echo in the Greek myth: "I confirm from here what you know from there."

K. Influencing your choice of early steps in the work is your conception of where the work is eventually going. *You* know that later activities will embrace science and will include the tasks of paper making, ink making, and possibly sharpening and writing with a quill feel they are ready for further probing with their "drama eyes," helped by all carrying out the *same* task.

Using manuscripts and books (*scholarly* texts, where possible, not watered down information) about monasteries, introduce the concept of *quills.* Suggest that the making of a quill is something every monk would be skilled in. Discuss what the stages of making would have to be. Invite them to strip and cut the quills. They may see this as "just" a miming exercise, but you know that it is the "quill in the head" that you are after and in order to help them find this, you may move into role as they work:

"Young brother, you will notice how finely strong the quill center of each feather is, how it tapers to the tip and bends and springs in the sure fingers of the experienced shaper. You must be certain that your blade is honed to sharpness and that your hands are steady upon the cutting board as you shape the tip to carry and hold the inks that will inscribe words to the Glory of God. Remember at this time your thoughts must not stray, your eyes not lift, nor your fingers falter in shaping this feather, which has been spared to us from one of God's creatures."

To avoid "merely miming" you could ask each child to record each process using words or sketches in a way that could be understood by *"novices who submit themselves to our calling."*

L. You may judge that the class are now ready to move naturally to individual tasks again. For example, mixing feed for the geese, pouring wines into skins or bottles, mixing and kneading bread, cleaning ovens, cutting and carrying wood, grinding herbs for medicines. Having observed their choices of duties, you may have prepared individual or group "task cards." The instruction card should be stylish in appearance, layout, and language, and the deliberate obscurity of language supplemented by the directness of the accompanying sketch. (An example is shown in Figure 4-2.)

(for *real,* because this is science and craft). So in this task while you are setting *now* in making quills with "drama eyes," you are anticipating the actual craft work they will do later out of role.

L. This procedure of recording everything done should be established early in the work. It is part of mantle of the expert's approach to identifying what has been learned and to self-evaluation.

Once students can make this start, you become extremely active. You, in your role as abbot, have the power to invade, patrol, and give and take information with a view to sustaining energy, building images, challenging some to go further, broadcasting any child's new thinking, and so on. It will help if the abbot has news to bring. The news should be quite mundane, not particularly exciting, and should be able to be qualified or biased according to the tasks the students are currently engaged in. For example, an "invented" brother may be in the infirmary and anxious that his work be covered in his absence. Approaching cellarers pouring wine, it may be imparted as: *"I have just been with Brother Cadfael in the infirmary. His leg is healing nicely, but he yearns for that horn of wine brother herbalist promised him after the tenth day. How is the mead standing, brothers? Are all the jars safely warmed in their woolen covers? Let me help you. . . ."* Talking with gardeners, it may emerge as *"You will be pleased to hear that Brother Cadfael's broken leg is knitting together well. He will soon require a crutch. He misses our companionship, and could then sit out here and watch you at work."* And to the swanherd

your task this day is to carve the horns of the devil Beelzebub upon the new mysericord in chapel so that in the early morning when brothers must be kept awake before dawn, the wood will support their leaning but not sitting, and the face of the Devil remind them of the power of evil to tempt the mind from prayer.

let the horns be cut deep and very pointed.

should the knife slip, be certain you have cloths to staunch any blood which may briefly flow.

Let the knife be sharp and well-pointed also to carve sharp and clean.

FIGURE 4-2. *A Possible Task Card Prepared in Advance by Teacher or Older Children.*

M. You are about to enter a new phase of the drama—introducing the bishop's letter. We suggest you do this first *out of role*. *"When we go back to being monks again, do you think we could cope with receiving a messenger—a messenger from the bishop! I've tried to make it look important by putting a seal on it. Don't open it yet until we're back in the drama, but see how it feels in your hand"* [pass it round for inspection]. *"Can we agree it's from the bishop? I've written it of course, but I've done my best to sound authoritative! No I'm not telling you what's in it* [with a smile, no doubt!]. *Now, how do you think the abbot will call everyone together for the opening of the letter? Ring a bell? Send one monk around to everyone? Open it at mealtime? Do we want to see the messenger hand it over? Who thinks they know how he would do it? Does he arrive on horseback?"*

You will be able to set the situation up using their suggestions, and the students will have begun to take responsibility for running their monastery.

it may be *"Can you show me the great male swan that broke Brother Cadfael's leg last month? It really must be a powerful bird! I told him he must have done something to irk the poor bird, but he swears he was only collecting pinion feathers as calmly as ever! What do you think may have caused the bird to be so aggressive?"* However, two things are important here. The teacher must not suggest that any group or individual monk/child is missing a colleague from the work team. And there *is* now a Brother Cadfael in the infirmary with a broken leg caused by the wing of a swan while he was collecting pinion feathers! Think of the curriculum prospects: prayers for healing; visits to the sick room; herbal medicines; the ways temporarily incapacitated people, normally strong, pass the hours while bones heal; ways of setting bones; the human skeleton; leverage; building crutches to take weight when wood and ropes and iron nails are the resource materials; using pulleys to keep a leg bone in place; diet for invalids; how to take your mind off pain; whether swans need forgiveness; composing the information about the accident in a letter to the bishop or prior; and so on.

M. Introducing the bishop's letter is going to provide the rest of the curriculum, so working toward at least some degree of "ownership" out of role, before the dramatic event takes place, may be essential: you therefore ask them for their agreement—a kind of verbal contract. They actually *handle* the letter and, of course, you "hook" their interest in its possible content. This letter provides the *dynamic* now for the rest of the mantle of the expert work. This chapter has been describing all the preliminary activities necessary before the "dynamic" can be introduced. How you will proceed from here will depend on the students' readiness to take on the mantle. We offer some ideas in the next chapter.

••

Progressing and Deepening the Work

A gradual move toward a degree of ownership is a necessary preface to the "hard" work on the curriculum that the teacher has in mind. Before moving to the Bishop's letter, let's consider another model that Dorothy Heathcote adopts for gauging student readiness for penetrating a topic more deeply.

A teacher has an obligation to develop the skill capacities, reasoning ability, and understanding of the students. In the case of the monastery, once the students are enjoying working on the daily tasks of monks, the teacher watches for opportunities to widen their horizons about monasteries generally, while at the same time narrowing the focus of the work to teach curriculum skills. Dorothy finds the circle of progression in Figure 4-3 particularly helpful in that each quarter provides a checklist for when the next progression can begin.

Each quarter of the circle represents the kind, degree, and quality of the students' engagement with an area of study. At first (top left-hand quartile) there is an exploratory "playing around" with whatever form the initial stimulus takes. In the second (top right-hand) segment, some implications are glimpsed and decisions about focus become necessary, so plans begin to emerge. In the third quartile the students begin to carry out the tasks, skills may need to be taught, and information needs to be accurate. In the final quarter, the work is consolidated by changing its perspective, not through repetition; confidence in their own newly acquired knowledge and skills sees the students through.

Thus each quarter forms part of a cyclic journey toward greater understanding, skill, and self-spectatorship. This does not happen by chance—it is a result of teacher intervention. Each time the teacher decides to move from one section to the next, he uses different language both in style and terminology: he sets parameters that will focus the work and create the opportunity for learning and practicing relevant skills. The work involved in acquiring this knowledge and these skills will create a readiness in the participants to develop further potential in tackling more complex work.

Thus the Circle of Progression not only *guides* the teacher in making the move from quarter to quarter but *regulates* the teacher's classroom resources—his language and demeanour and the kinds of support or challenges he provides. Figure 4-4, shows a circle of progression relative to the bishop's letter in the monastery scenario. Sometimes the four quarters will be entered and left quite quickly over a short period of time. On other occasions, each quarter will be lingered in because of the momentous or complex nature of the

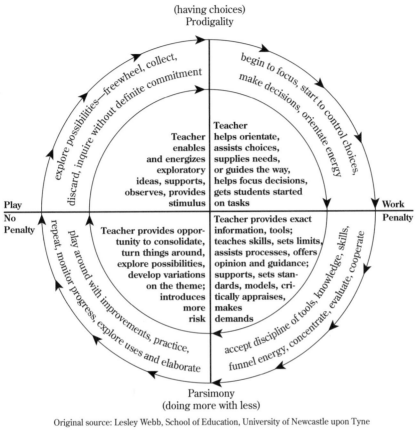

(having choices)
Prodigality

begin to focus, start to control choices, make decisions, orientate energy

explore possibilities—freewheel, collect, discard, inquire without definite commitment

Teacher
enables
and energizes
exploratory
ideas, supports,
observes, provides
stimulus

Teacher
helps orientate,
assists choices,
supplies needs,
or guides the way,
helps focus decisions,
gets students started
on tasks

Play
No
Penalty

Work
Penalty

Teacher provides oppor-
tunity to consolidate,
turn things around,
explore possibilities,
develop variations
on the theme;
introduces
more
risk

Teacher provides exact
information, tools;
teaches skills, sets limits,
assists processes, offers
opinion and guidance;
supports, sets stan-
dards, models, cri-
tically appraises,
makes
demands

repeat, monitor progress, explore uses and elaborate

play around with improvements, practice,

accept discipline of tools, knowledge, skills, evaluate, cooperate

funnel energy, concentrate, evaluate, cooperate

Parsimony
(doing more with less)

Original source: Lesley Webb, School of Education, University of Newcastle upon Tyne

FIGURE 4-3. *The Circle of Progression. Each time a line is crossed a teacher shifts gear, language, pace, vocabulary.*

work. The teacher will have to decide the pace guided by observations of the students' cognitive readiness and expectations of learning in school. In traditional teaching, students are often thrust quickly into the third quarter of the work with little orientation received in the first and second quarters. Also, the fourth quarter of consolidation and maturation is often taken for granted and just left to chance.

Introducing the Bishop's Letter

With the circle of progression in mind, Dorothy now plans how the bishop's letter might be used to extend and deepen the students' understanding and skills. The introduction of a letter from Bishop Anselm, written by his secretary, is a device to further many of your ideas regarding curriculum areas to be worked on, for it provides

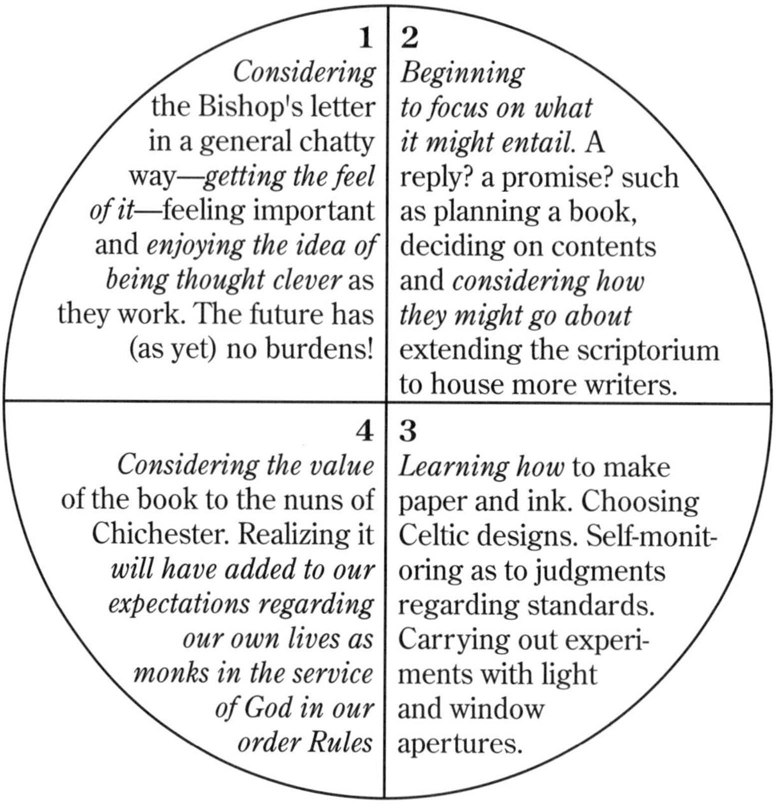

1
Considering the Bishop's letter in a general chatty way—*getting the feel of it*—feeling important and *enjoying the idea of being thought clever* as they work. The future has (as yet) no burdens!

2
Beginning to focus on what it might entail. A reply? a promise? such as planning a book, deciding on contents and *considering how they might go about* extending the scriptorium to house more writers.

4
Considering the value of the book to the nuns of Chichester. Realizing it *will have added to our expectations regarding our own lives as monks in the service of God in our order Rules*

3
Learning how to make paper and ink. Choosing Celtic designs. Self-monitoring as to judgments regarding standards. Carrying out experiments with light and window apertures.

FIGURE 4-4. *Progression Circle for Bishop's letter exercise.*

the dynamic that will move all subsequent work forward with a strong sense of purpose. Let us assume you have written the letter with specific science curriculum areas in mind: you want to teach certain aspects of the science of light, and you want the children to understand how paper is made. (The student teacher confined herself to the making of paper as her science objective.)

Inescapably, decisions now have to be made with regard to the letter's request: (1) how to reply to the request in the proper way; (2) how to revise the present monastery ground plan to accommodate an extended scriptorium in which all of the monks can work on the book at once; and (3) how to determine which rules to pass along to the nuns.

You are thus faced with a typical drama dilemma. So often, actors in drama are required to *pretend* to make a decision—the actor playing Othello pretends to decide to kill Desdemona, for example. Although you want the class (for the sake of your curriculum planning) to agree to make the book and to extend the scriptorium in order to achieve the extra workspace, you want them to give some thought to the *implications* behind such a contract—for the monks, that is. The chances are you will get a glib "Okay, we'll agree" or a "We can't do it. We're too busy with our jobs."

Therefore, let's think about the kinds of tactics you can employ to give the class time to identify some of the criteria the monks would be bound to employ when faced with such a letter. However you handle it, you must *delay* decision making. *Pondering*—either in or out of role—on what is at issue is what is required. Because your students will not sufficiently "own" their monastery lifestyle at this point, they will find it very difficult to grasp the possible implications.

However, they are likely to pick up the *affective* connotations of a remark like the following, made in your role as abbot—*"I think I should warn you that the making of the book will tax our powers to the utmost. It will mean long hours in the scriptorium, yet beasts must be fed, bread made and offices sung just as we always do"*—particularly if it is balanced with: *"Brothers, I have heard only good of Bishop Anselm, and it is said that he is wise in business matters as well as vigilant in prayer."*

On the other hand, *out* of role, you might muse: *"You do wonder how monks would think about a bishop they've never met"* or *"I suppose they might have vows they take to obey their bishop. Does the letter sound like a command?"*

From all this it is quite obvious that any input from the teacher in verbal discourse influences greatly the kind of language and thinking emerging from the students. In spite of your efforts to raise the level of their decision making you may find yourself with a class (as the student teacher did) who simply want to get on with the practicalities of changing the shape of their scriptorium. However, if your students are beginning to engage with the issue at a deeper level, then you have a variety of options to choose from:

1. Establish with the students that:

    a. As they get on with other schoolwork, they will jot down on a big piece of paper why they think helping the bishop is a good idea, or
    b. As they continue their monastic duties in role, they will enter the scriptorium when they feel ready to write what they think should be done.

2. If you feel confident that the children have the social skills to handle the decision themselves, suggest that as the monks go about their tasks they can discuss the book and how they want to respond to the bishop's letter. This would require a notice to be prepared (out of role) by the class and you to remind the monks of the various aspects of the letter that need to be considered:

    ▪ The grant of monies to pay for the extension
    ▪ Problems of rebuilding/equipping new space
    ▪ The urgency of the task
    ▪ Skills the brothers do or don't possess
    ▪ Reorganization of duties
    ▪ Coping with extra visitors
    ▪ Training extra novices.

    This list clearly signals that there can be no quick decisions, that the monks need to start thinking about *all* the implications that must be discussed at the next meeting. At this time you as Abbot would be working alongside the monks, both giving conscientious support to whatever their immediate tasks demanded and noting at what level they are considering the challenge from the bishop.

3. Ask the students to hold a ballot or a public vote *out of role* after they have discussed the advice they would give the monks about various points of the letter. Every teacher knows about the hazards of peer pressure in such debates, but that is a risk worth taking if there are also advantages.

There are as many possibilities as there are inventive teachers as to how the decision can be taken, but the most important point in teaching (not only in mantle of the expert work) is that understanding is brought about by a process of engagement.

Drafting a Reply to the Bishop's Letter

Whichever method you choose, you and your class will reach the point when a *reply* to the bishop will need to be written. Again, you have a wide choice of strategies available to you. The actual task of bringing the letter into being will depend entirely on what processes you wish the students to experience.

One method is (as the abbot) to tinkle a bell during work to announce that the matter of what to put in the reply will be discussed over repast *("We will need to order our thoughts . . ")* and, as they are eating (or whatever mutual activity has been negotiated), to lead the conversation directly to debating the pros and cons of their reply, possibly writing down (having contracted that a modern felt-tip pen can be used in place of a quill or stylus) the statements they agree on. You would thus be a scribe, taking dictation, reading back to them their decisions until you feel they've *"had enough for now"* or need more time to ponder.

Another system may be that each monk (or small group) composes a first draft. The whole group then reads them over (there are many interesting ways to arrange this!) and makes selections for the final reply.

A final suggestion is that the abbot be allowed, with the assistance of two or three brothers (slow learners?), to prepare the letter, make copies, and take them around to all the brother monks for agreement.

At this point everyone can decide how the final scribing will be accomplished. For example, some students may need the honor of being entrusted to pen the final letter. They may be the ones who need writing practice or confidence or to face a big responsibility.

Focusing on the Scriptorium

It will be obvious by now that in the mantle of the expert kind of teaching each individual, working in the space available—whether classroom, hall, or corridor—develops an internal sense of his or her own functioning territory that has nothing to do with actual space. This inner image transforms all the actual surroundings and objects, and the children develop "avoidance skills" as they work in close proximity. This includes conventions such as not catching another's eye unless a consultation is required and not bumping into others who are also working internally and having different mind perceptions even though they are sharing the same desk space.

However, some images must be forged in common in order to give limits to the work. It would be ridiculous for monastic architectural style to be left open! So you must decide in advance on what cannot be left to chance. In this case, you have presented two givens: the bishop's letter and the monastery ground plan. A further word now needs to be said about the latter.

The plan must be large enough so the entire class can see it but small enough to be easily storable and accessible. It also has to allow for modifications to be added. Such a plan would normally include the artist's name who did the drawings, orientation compass points, and an indication of previous alterations from an earlier time. How elaborate these signs need be here depend on your preparation time and how authentic a 'feel' you want to create. You need to be sure that this particular plan includes:

1. The compass orientation (correct for monastic chapel conventions). This is essential because of the science/"light" work you intend to introduce as part of the curriculum.
2. A smallish scriptorium, one that is obviously too small for all the monks to fit into.
3. Spaces into which an addition can be fitted.
4. Correct labeling and terminology (e.g., *refectory, dormitory, scriptorium*) An earlier step could have been to teach these names to novices. This *does not require more students;* in fact, it is essential there are no actual novices to be taught! Planting the idea of novices is quite sufficient to make a proper, *imperative* reason to labeling plans and name buildings correctly *"so that novices can find their way about."*
5. A systematic, consistent scale for all parts of the plan.

In starting the work of giving close study to the plan, you will have to appreciate that students of this age may have had little if any exposure to this form of representation. If they find it quite difficult to translate lines on paper into stone buildings, then they are even more unlikely to visualize stone buildings with rooms, and rooms with windows through which light variably shines. You will have to give careful thought to how you are going to initiate them into these skills. Even such an obvious matter as where best to place the plan in the classroom should be considered carefully: on the floor? on the wall? on a table? There are pros and cons for each:

- On the floor: plan can more easily be destroyed
  plan will hold attention—all can see it move around it, and talk across it easily it will feel like ours; we're in charge of it
- On the wall: plan safe but distant
  will be talked *about*
  plan will dominate but be more difficult to own
  appropriate for intimate, small-group discussions, but it

will be difficult to find a "public voice" in class discussion
without standing in front of it
little contact between back and front positions
- On a table: demands understanding of "taller people at
  back" the "pushers" will tend to "hog" the perimeter of
  table
  plan will become owned only if spatial problems are
  settled first.

Alternative ways of presenting the plan include slides, elevated models, or "jigsaw" cutouts, each one having its own advantages and
drawbacks.

Whatever device is used, when you gather around the plan, you
need to prompt the class to:

1. Interpret the lines on the paper as representing buildings
   in which people can move about and work.
2. Translate the various signs into information: scale
   dimensions, compass directions, inside/outside areas.
3. Identify the scriptorium, its relation to other places, and its
   entrances and exits.
4. Discuss what the scriptorium might have inside it at the
   moment and how many monks it could house (*at work*) at
   any one time.
5. Develop a realization that light matters (for good or ill
   regarding inks, eyes, parchment) and conceptualize
   aperture shapes, wall thicknesses, and seasonal
   temperatures, particularly as they affect the comfort of
   hands and feet.
6. Realize that walls are thick and stones and mortar are
   heavy and inanimate; that some walls must be taken down
   and others put up; and that humans are vulnerable when
   using ladders, weights, and pulleys!
7. Realize that changing buildings requires money: new
   materials have to be located and transported.
8. Realize that walls are more than outside shapes: they
   create a living and working space and generally help to
   create the ambience of a monk's life.

You will decide how far into all the above your initial discussions
should penetrate, but as the abbot you will constantly be drawing
attention to *our* work, *our* dimensions, *our* tools, *our* skills. This

ownership leads very naturally to those science and mathematics areas so important to the teacher. There is a vested interest in checking what *I* can see if the sun is in *my* eyes; how *my* papers will curl if left in direct sunshine; how *my* quill will roll away in dark corners if work benches slope too much; how *my* feet will chill if the door does not fit well; or how fire may consume *us all* if safe distances for paper, logs, robes, are not attended to with care. This also involves action—it will not be a smooth abstract discussion, but will require frequent stops to pace out sizes, use measuring wheels and tapes, estimate the spaces and heights scribes require so as not to disturb each other. Different groups or individual monks may explore, under the abbot's guidance, many different aspects simultaneously.

The Science of Light

For much of this work, you will need to move, *out* of role, into "normal" science practice with second or third grade—measuring shadows in the playground at different times of the day; examining the classroom for light and dark areas; examining the effect of sunlight on skin and on other surfaces; investigating the effect seasonal changes have on sunlight; testing whether thickness as well as height and width of window openings makes a difference in the amount and quality of light admitted; directing light to paper through a magnifying glass; textbook explanations of light phenomena where appropriate. This will all of course be done within the context of *"we will need to know for the sake of the work to be done in our monastery."*

It will be necessary for you to make a model (with suitably thick walls and window openings) based on the agreed plan of the enlarged scriptorium, but first you may want to find out the extent of the students' present understanding of concepts related to light. One way to do this is to lay out two large sheets of paper on tables in different parts of the room. One sheet is to be labeled, I *know* this to be true about light shining through windows, the other, I *think* this is true about light shining through windows. (With older students, you might consider including a third category, I *believe* this to be true.) The students will write on either of these sheets as they think fit, or you in some cases may do the writing to their dictation.

Everyone should then gather around the "know" table and together decide whether the statements are accurate. This allows you to check the quality of their understanding. Items known to be true will be indicated in some way chosen by the class, the uncertainties left unmarked. No attempt should be made, at this stage, to inform or to grade their efforts; it is a matter of getting the children to confirm their own thinking and to decide as a group about its accuracy. You too can occasionally add your thoughts, the kind that open up possibilities rather than close doors with superior knowledge. For instance, tucked in a bottom corner the children may find, "I know light can affect my mood." When everyone moves over to the *"think"* table, it may be decided that some of the items could be transferred to the *"know"* list. Then perhaps a third sheet will be prepared listing "things we need to find out about." This leads to closer examination of library resources and textbooks.

Where appropriate, a formal scientific experiment, again moving away from the monastery fiction for a while, can directly anticipate the scriptorium problem. Have the students build a three-dimensional model out of cardboard of a room shaped similarly to the scriptorium. It should include thick window embrasures and a figure (*not* a monk) to give a sense of the scale. Ask the students what advice they would give to the curators of this art gallery, *drawing on their new knowledge about the science of light,* about the effect of sunshine at different times of the day and year on both the room and on the pictures that will hang in it? They will thus be required to apply their knowledge (no doubt using a flashlight to represent sunlight through windows at different angles) in the special way that will be needed for their drama.

Gradually, you will shift your musing about these scientific matters and their present-day application to wondering aloud *"how much those monks would know of what we know"* and why they would know it. This not only introduces the students to the concept of the historical progression of scientific knowledge but also eases them back into their role as monks.

They are now in a position once more to look closely at the model, this time as their scriptorium, and to impress the abbot with the model *"they have brought along."* As the abbot, you will play the innocent: *"How can we test the degree and angles of light that will enter the windows?"* If your musings have been effective, the students will realize that in their demonstration to the abbot, candles will have to replace the flashlight. (If school insurance prohibits using a lighted candle in the classroom, you and the class, out of role, will have to agree that a flashlight can "stand in.") *Monk* figures can be introduced to give a sense of scale, and the light moved according to the compass orientation. Experiments with scriptorium furniture (benches and desks) in different parts of the room in relation to the sunlight will focus their attention on monks at work. Their findings will then be written up. A visit from another teacher, a parent, or the principal (in role as a visitor staying overnight?) who asks them to explain what they are doing would provide an incentive to reinforce their learning.

What Next?

You have reached an important stage in the work when you and your class will have to agree that the renovations have been completed. In the above section we have given detailed attention to the lighting problems affecting the scriptorium extension, but you might prefer to concentrate on building materials, the construction of walls and roof, etc. Or you may do both.

It is important to note here that the "normal" miming actions of imitating the building of an extension become superfluous. The extension is built *symbolically* through the detailed attention to lighting or building materials. The *activities* are sophisticated ones of grappling with some scientific, architectural, or mathematical problem, *not* pretending to grapple with stones. That is not to say that miming actions are always inappropriate—we earlier suggested such actions for the monks going about their duties—but it will be discovered that in a mantle of the expert approach, the deeper the students get into the topic, the less they will feel the need to demonstrate routine actions to each other in order to get into their roles. Exploring the ramifications of an angle of light will bring the extension of the scriptorium into being more effectively than miming the effort of heaving heavy stones. The drama is in the *mind*. On the other hand, if the emphasis for some reason was to be about illuminators of mediaeval script turning their artistic hands to heaving stones, then the detailed examination of those miming actions may become critical to the project. In fact, in the student teacher's version of the work, building the extension was mimed. But in that instance, the science of paper making became the central activity. Building the extension was secondary, and *token* miming actions were all that were needed to reach a point of agreement with the class that *"the new scriptorium is now ready."*

Whatever route you take, the time will arrive when the monks will experience their new scriptorium for the first time; whether this entails recording the changes and what it feels like to be spending so much time writing in addition to other duties or having a ceremony blessing the extension or simply rearranging the desks will depend on the emphasis you feel is right for your particular class. In fact we are reaching the point in the plan where it is no longer possible to anticipate just how and when you complete the project of writing the book of rules and hand it over to the bishop's representative. And of course, the *manner* of handing it over presents you with yet another set of options.

The next stage of the science work, paper making, together with the creating the book and the handing it over, will be included in the student teacher's account that follows. First, however, we need to draw attention to a curious paradox related to actuality as a productive stimulus for the fiction.

The Third Track: Actuality

A significant shift has occurred during our previous science work on light. In the early stages of mantle of the expert work, you and the students were following the single track of creating a monastery (i.e., running an enterprise) by representing the monks' labors, labors that were never carried out *in actuality*—they were simulated or written about or talked about. You then superimposed a *second track* of dealing with the implications of the bishop's (i.e., the client's) letter: "superimposed," because in moving along the new track one still had to keep going on the first track of monastery duties. To create the second track, dramatic metaphor is again the medium: there is not *an actual* letter from a bishop, nor does a scriptorium get built. The mantle of the expert device adopted for the first track is used to create a context for the various curriculum matters of the second.

But when these two tracks have been firmly established, when they are owned by the children as well as by the teacher, then, at suitable times, a third track of *actuality* can be followed in a way that paradoxically enhances the *nonactuality* of the first two tracks. We are referring here to activities such as going out into the playground to measure shadows or looking at the effect of a prism on light, which are of course carried out in a nonfictional mode but which implicitly or explicitly are being done *"for the sake of what we need to know in our monastery work."* Likewise, in your next scientific work on making paper, much time will be spent out of role *in the service of* the in-role work, for the children *in actuality* are going to make paper. This may at first appear to contradict a golden rule that emerged in the earlier chapters, that in the mantle of the expert approach everything is done symbolically: if you are running a shoe factory, you do not actually make shoes. And certainly if we were running a paper factory, we would not make paper, at least not in the initial stages of developing ownership, for the owning process depends on symbolic mediation.

However, once the shoe factory or the monastery is *owned,* the third track of actuality becomes yet another way of proceeding and you will find yourself using this kind of dialogue with the class: *"If we need our monks to make the book, we'll have to get the paper made, so that when we work in our scriptorium we'll have the proper sort of paper, won't we?"* And musing about *"what should be the first words we write on our paper?"* may well take place while the students are waiting for the paper to dry, as a way to foreshadow the excitement of being almost ready to write the book of monastery rules.

We will see in just a moment that a form of actuality the student teacher used was to invite a real monk into the classroom. Since she set the occasion up straightforwardly as having her students ask the monk questions, this was clearly using the third track. If, more productively perhaps, the visiting friar had entered the make-believe and, without patronizing, treated the students as colleague friars, then the first track would have been followed.

Where Have We Been?

The above account has covered several weeks' work. For the students the central thrust of the experience is "working in a mediaeval monastery." For the teacher the monastery idea ia a *baseline* from which the whole curriculum can be developed. Only if the teacher is able from the beginning of the project to visualize it in terms of *curriculum learning* will the full potential of mantle of the expert approach be realized.

The teacher's planning must therefore ensure that many levels of knowledge and skills *across* the curriculum will be tapped. They fall into two kinds:

1. Aspects of knowledge/skill that are integral to the context chosen (Obviously, with "mediaeval monastery" we are into history and religion, but decisions still have to be made about *which* aspects of history and religion); and
2. Aspects of knowledge/skill for which the teacher has to *contrive* a need, a need that must logically and emotionally stem from the monastery work but that is not specific to the monastery context (for example, in this case problems in science, technology, and math having to do with extending a room).

Since the knowledge and skills in 2 have to feel emotionally as well as logically right to the pupils, the choice of what and how is very important. The chart in Figure 4-5 shows that more than half the curriculum work sprang from the "contrivance" of the bishop's letter. Without that letter there would have been considerably less English and virtually no science or math. In Chapter 2 we referred to the need to provide a *dynamic* that will give the whole work impetus. We are now in a position to see that the central thrust of such a dynamic is in the direction of curriculum areas. The bishop's letter provides the *necessity* for learning about sunlight and paper making and the social strata of the church and language styles, and as the work proceeds the pupils will recognize that more and more they will be

Episode	Task/s	Role in	Role out	Role both	Language	Art	Craft/Design	Mathematics	Sciences	Religious Educ.	History	Georgrahpy	Music	Physical Educ.
examining cards	read/discuss		✓		✓					✓	✓			
work of monks	" " + match		✓		✓					✓	✓			
teacher reads duties of monks	self correct		✓		✓					✓	✓			
visualizing work	personal images		✓		✓					✓	✓			
telling a friend	hearing + visualizing		✓		✓					✓	✓			
speaking for friend	interpreting and amplifying		✓		✓									
choosing work	taking decisions		✓		✓									
examining plan of monastery	codes. scale. space. orientation		✓	✓✓	✓	✓	✓	✓		✓	✓			
starting work	symbolic active behavior as monks	✓											✓	✓
Bishop's letter	contract to the fictional truth			✓✓	✓					✓	✓			
monastic work	demonstrating work	✓			✓					✓	✓		✓	✓
consulting plan once more	review and reconsider alternatives			✓✓	✓	✓		✓	✓	✓	✓			
replying to the letter	order thinking	✓	✓	✓✓	✓									
modeling the scriptorium	shaping, measuring with accuracy		✓		✓			✓	✓	✓	✓			
testing light and shadows	experimenting		✓	✓✓	✓	✓	✓	✓	✓	✓	✓	✓		
explaining the new scriptorium	defining what they know to themselves	✓	✓	✓✓	✓	✓	✓	✓	✓	✓	✓	✓		
papermaking	different shapes and process		✓		✓			✓	✓	✓		✓		
writing the book selected tools	exploring texts space on paper		✓			✓	✓	✓	✓	✓	✓			

FIGURE 4-5. *Systematic Scale.*

working *out* of role, in order to master aspects of the curriculum. They will become as immersed in normal curriculum tasks as in any traditional classroom—reading texts and theoretical works, writing notes, carrying out experiments, etc. But we believe that through the mantle of the expert the *quality* of their studies will be enhanced.

The "what and how" of the dynamic are central to the teacher's planning. If the bishop's letter feels right to the pupils, then virtually anything can follow—for several weeks! Such a choice and its presentation needs meticulous planning.

There will be other aspects of the work, however, that cannot be so carefully planned beforehand—the aspects that need to be *negotiated* with the students. For instance, it can be a matter of discussion with the class whether, having made their own paper, they want to try writing something on it right away—and if so what?—or they want to wait until they have worked out *what* rules they want to advise the bishop of.

To some extent you will have an idea of where the work is likely to go—it is no exaggeration to say that a key to the art of teaching lies in the teacher's ability to *anticipate,* and to *foreshadow* in one learning activity what will be needed in a subsequent learning activity. It is rather like the playwright who plants in Act 1 a piece of information that will make sense to the audience in Act 3. Just as the audience can make connections when the time is right, so children can take advantage of the *cumulative* process of acquiring knowledge/skills. We have a concrete example in our plan where the teacher, conscious that the monks' ability to read two-dimensional plans is going to be critical, gives the pupils practice in looking at the plan of the monastery, testing their ability in this respect, in the very early stages of the project *before* those abilities become essential (i.e., irreversibly harnessed to the reexamination of the plan with a view to extending the scriptorium).

It is often useful for a teacher to classify the different kinds of learning to be aimed at. The chart in Figure 4-5 shows how, as the monastery lessons develop, the students become increasingly involved in work across more and more curriculum areas. The *intensity* and *kind* of the involvement will depend upon the teacher's concerns at any particular time—for instance, whether the academic or affective has priority.

Take the episode of the monks' examining the ground plan of their monastic buildings, for example. The teacher must decide, in discussing matters such as the scriptorium extension, the location of the gardens, the importance of hospitality, and geographical detail,

(a) whether (and how strongly) to push for public or private discussions, (b) how much technical vocabulary she will model, (c) how many and what kind of note-taking opportunities to provide for groups or individuals, and (d) how far historical concepts or sacred/secular distinctions will be considered.

Whatever decisions the teacher makes, one thing she is always teaching is that all change has consequences and that those consequences require close examination. Each episode contains some "seeding" of the next challenge, and the progression from one *lesson* to another will relate with the coherent development from one task to another.

In Figure 4-5, the labels for the curriculum areas cover many skills that the teacher will further break down into discrete components. For instance, "language" will encapsulate "talking," "reading," and "writing" at a first level, but these, in turn, will break down further. Talking, for instance, involves the social skills of discussing privately or publicly and of asking or answering questions. These are further broken down into abilities in language, speech, and voice techniques. All curriculum skills can be subdivided in this way. The art of using a mantle of the expert approach lies in selecting just the right task to meet the precisely identified skill.

Student Teacher Uses the Monastery Topic

(This account is written by Marianne Heathcote, Dorothy's daughter, about an experience that took place a few years ago. She feels she would now do some things rather differently, but it is useful, for the purposes of this book, to see how a student teacher set about using a mantle of the expert approach.)

During my first practice teaching assignment, I visited an elementary school one day a week for the first semester, then conducted a three-week teaching block in January. The students were seven to nine years old and the topic was "Mediaeval Monastery."

The major aim of the three-week segment was for the students to produce a book that showed their understanding of how life was for monks in those times. As far as I could see, I had two options: the students could read some books from the library service collection and make notes and pictures from them about life in a mediaeval monastery, or they could behave as if they were real monks running a monastery and then, *in role,* write about how life in the monastery *is.*

The second idea seemed more appealing, since it would not be just an exercise in note taking but a real expression of what the students had come to understand. They would be more clearly motivated to write about their own experiences than to copy from books. So I chose to run a mantle of the expert project.

I don't know much theory about the mantle of the expert style of teaching, but what I do know, I know from gut reactions, from having been taught from an early age in classes of children "doing" mantle of the expert, and from seeing Dorothy at work. My very basic understanding of the process is that the students should be *running* some sort of project, in which they are in role, and that they should have a high degree of autonomy, not be "talked down to" by a teacher speaking as a fount of wisdom. I based my mediaeval monastery project on these two basic ideas.

A number of set assignments from my university were to be incorporated into my practice teaching. Two of them, religious education and science, linked readily with my mantle of the expert project. For the former I was required to take the class to a sacred building, so I chose Durham Cathedral, which had once been a monastery; for the latter, which was to be based on the concept of *change,* I opted for paper making, which fitted logically into my monastery theme.

The first lesson, the day before the trip to Durham Cathedral, lasted one and a half hours. The intention was not to throw the children directly into the drama, expecting them to behave in role as monks, but to give them an initial exercise introducing the tasks that were carried out in a mediaeval monastery. I had prepared twenty-eight cards, fourteen of them naming typical monastery tasks and a matching fourteen giving brief definitions or "job descriptions." The students had to pair up the cards: the task with its appropriate description.

One lot of cards read:

Cellarers; Keeper of Relics; Refectorians; Chamberlains; Almoners; Master of Novices; Infirmarians; Psalmist; Herbalist and Gardener; Kitchener; Flockmaster; Guest-master; Sacristans; Precentors.

The other cards read:

In charge of the cellars and store-food, ale and wine; Looks after the ancient remains of saints and their shrines; Looks after linen, bedding, hot water, fire, shoes, habits and shaving heads; Cares for the poor, providing food, clothing and shelter; In charge of

teaching lessons; Looks after medicines, first aid, operations and
infirmary building; In charge of music, singing, choir books and
the Church bell; In charge of the plants and herbs and making
inks; in charge of the cooking; Looks after animals such as
geese (to make quills for writing) and hens, cows and sheep;
Looks after visiting pilgrims and their horses; Looks after
contents of Church, vestments, banners, books and vessels at
the altar; In charge of organizing Church services and choosing
readings from Holy Books. Also in charge of cloisters.

The students all looked at the cards and discussed them. Whenever
a child thought she had made a pair, she showed them to me, and
we put them together on the wall. I also put up my own large labeled
plan of the monastery, which conveyed the sense that each of the
fourteen tasks was *based* somewhere in the monastery (there were
herb gardens, a kitchen, an infirmary, etc).

We had a discussion about what to call the monastery. The children were torn between two saints' names and eventually decided to
call it The Monastery of Saints. I now gave out a set of "qualities"
on cards—"being able to listen carefully to what others think," "being
able to repair things," "not neglecting things even when I don't feel
like doing things," etc. Working in pairs, the students considered
these qualities, looking at the pairs of cards they had put on display
and thinking about which jobs would need which qualities. I stressed
all the time that there were no right or wrong answers and that each
quality did not have to be matched with a particular task. Then we
discussed the jobs and qualities as a class.

Lastly, I asked the children to consider what we had discussed,
think about what qualities *they* had, and write down which task they
thought that they would be good at doing. (Although I asked them
to do this without consulting their friends, many of them did so
anyway; but there were also a number of children who did not speak
to others about their choice.) Later, when I looked at the papers the
students handed in concerning the tasks they thought they would
be good at, nine of the fourteen jobs had been chosen.

Looking back at the lesson, I felt that the students had not been
afraid to speak out and that the discussion had gone well: no one
seemed bored or tired and they hadn't polarized over naming the
monastery. I felt the lesson as a whole had achieved its aim of getting
the children interested and involved in a mediaeval monastery and
what went on there. I had asked them a lot of questions about the
tasks and what they would entail, and had asked them to use their
imagination. I was pleased that both boys and girls showed equal

interest and enthusiasm in the monastery work and that no mention was made of *girls* in the class choosing tasks as *male* monks.

The next day, the class, with carefully prepared worksheets in hand, visited Durham Cathedral in the morning and an exhibition in the cathedral undercroft in the afternoon. Both activities fitted in closely with the mantle of the expert work, but the afternoon in the undercroft in particular, motivated them to use their observations in the later drama work.

Later in the week I had my second lesson, again an hour and a half, during which I hoped the students would begin to believe in the drama and get a group spirit. I began by asking the class to rest with their heads on their desks; when I touched them, they were to wake up in the monastery as monks. (I had previously seen their class teacher use this technique with them.) As the children started taking on their roles in the monastery, I helped them by encouraging them to get down to doing a job they had been putting off for a while, giving examples such as repairing a thatch, polishing vessels, checking apple stores, making some new ink. The students took to the roles extremely well; two of the boys who were "novice masters" explained to me at one point that they would have to go to preach in local villages, telling how good the monastery was, because novices were in short supply.

In order to unify the group before I presented them with the scroll from Bishop Anselm, I called them together for Holy Communion. We came to the carpet reverently in silence and passed around imaginary bread and wine (I had discarded Dorothy's idea of using paper drawings). The communion went very well and achieved the aim of creating a group spirit. The atmosphere was excellent! The lesson ended with the arrival of the bishop's scroll saying he was starting a convent in Chichester, and as he had heard they were great artists and calligraphers, he wanted them, while realizing they would probably have to extend their scriptorium, to make a book for the new nuns telling them about life in the monastery.

I see the letter as a central core of the work: by telling them things about themselves, it put them in role as monks with these skills—the children accepted the information about their being expert artists and calligraphers. They were then presented with a request to use these skills and to pass their understanding of mediaeval monasteries on to others (the convent nuns, through the medium of the book they were to produce).

The whole project hung on the letter from the bishop: first, it produced experts, and second, it set the task through which the students would show their learning and understanding. Of course the children were not *really* experts at this stage, but over the next two weeks they developed their understanding of monasteries and were able to write a book from their "firsthand" experiences as mediaeval monks. In explaining their work to others—that is, writing the book—the students came to understand the work better themselves, which I understand to be something central to mantle of the expert.

The next lesson, again an hour-and-a-half session, took place a couple of afternoons later. The intention was to organize the scriptorium extension work, as mentioned in the letter, using the funding provided by Bishop Anselm, and, if necessary, to draw plans. Another aim was for the students to work as a team in organizing the scriptorium extension and to treat the drama as real. At no stage did the children ever dress up in costume. We did use the occasional prop—I had a bell that I used to start chapter meetings in which the decisions were made, and it helped the children get into their roles—but the children were never involved in any dressing up. The students took to role very well in building the extension, and everybody was actively involved. Some students organized a group to build the foundations, which involved them in a lot of mimed manual work, while others worked on the glass for the windows and fitted them in. The latter team was led by a girl who had looked closely at windows in the museum in the undercroft at Durham Cathedral, and could explain to the others exactly how windows should be made. After the extension had been made (through their miming actions), the children started their written work about their tasks in the monastery. Although the occasional student copied something out of the books about monasteries, this happened very rarely. (I suggested such copying was perhaps wasteful of their valuable time!)

The students also produced their own set of rules for life (and their behavior) in the monastery, which they wrote on the blackboard, and later copied down into their book for the nuns:

1. Be quiet
2. Write silently
3. Always stop when the bell rings
4. Do not disturb the abbot (my role) when he is talking
5. Always be careful
6. Care and be kind
7. Do not shout
8. Do not run

The following two afternoons we started on the paper making. Because the paper was going into the book for the nuns of Chichester, they had real motivation to produce good work. The process of paper making was not, of course, done in role and did not involve mantle of the expert drama, but it did meet the science assignment I had been set on the concept of "Change." I gave the students a plastic-covered card containing clearly written procedures for how to make paper, and they filled in worksheets at various stages in the process documenting all the *changes* they observed taking place in the making of paper. By the second day we had got the consistency of the paper pulp just right. All we had to do now was leave it to dry and set over the next couple of days and the weekend, before the arduous task of peeling the sheets of the new paper off the newspaper it had dried on would begin!

The next afternoon the students looked at slides of the illuminated letters found in the Irish Book of Kells, a copy of the four Gospels in Latin, written in the ninth century A.D. They also looked at a copy of the Book of Kells, the Lindisfarne Gospels, and a book of Celtic designs. I wanted them to find out about different styles of illuminated lettering dating from medieval times. We looked at a lot of details in the lettering, to give ideas before the students created their own illuminated lettering for the book they were creating for the nuns. (The illuminated lettering the children produced did use Celtic designs, which they did not know about before that afternoon.)

The next piece of work for the monastery involved the children in looking at books, cards, and posters depicting medieval stained-glass windows. The girl who had looked into the making of windows while in Durham Cathedral undercroft also reminded the class about what she had discovered about windows. The children then mixed the three primary colours, plus white, to create their own paintings of stained-glass windows, to further illustrate the book they were producing for the Chichester nuns.

Using the paper they had made the previous week, the students next had to produce some illuminated manuscripts for the book. I hoped writing on paper they had made themselves rather than on standard, mass-produced white paper would cause them to take more care, to think carefully about what they wrote and how neatly they wrote it. I also hoped using this paper and writing with real sharpened quills would make the past more real to them.

We began with the students waking up in the monastery and having a chapter meeting. A child whose monastery job was the precentor gave us Holy Communion, and then the manuscript writing started. The students tried to write with the quills, but it was not particularly successful, so some ended up writing with black calligraphic pens, the rest with plain blue ballpoints. Despite this, the students loved writing on their own paper, and put a lot of effort into their work. Some copied out Bible passages or a Celtic poem, others chose passages from some of the books I had in class. The standard of the copying was very high, and considering the children had no previous experience with anything remotely like this, I was very impressed indeed.

When the book was finished, I took it to be bound. The students called it *The Book of Saints: A Book for the Nuns of Chichester, by the Monastery of Saints,* and it now contained the following, all of which had been written *twice* by the children, first in draft and then in neat copy on their homemade paper:

A title page
A dedication to the nuns of Chichester, including all the brothers' signatures
Plans of the Monastery of Saints and the local village, with each part of the monastery labeled with technical terminology
Detailed information about each of the jobs and tasks undertaken by each monk
Illuminated letters of each monk's name
Prayers written by the monks for the nuns of Chichester
Monastic rules of the Monastery of Saints
Paintings of stained-glass windows.

On the last day of my practice teaching, an exmonk came into the class to talk to the children about his life in a monastery. This was not mantle of the expert work, but a more traditional educational setup in which the students were free to ask questions. I found it particularly useful, and it rounded off the three weeks' work very well. In the afternoon assembly the students had the opportunity to show to the rest of the school the book they had produced, but most important of all, the teacher of the class that I had been working with attended a chapter meeting in role as the messenger of the Bishop of Chichester, to receive the great honor of the book that had been prepared so carefully for the nuns of Chichester. Thus the work ended, as it had started, full of purpose and meaning.

Scandal, Disease, and Death! A Teacher's Nightmare?

■ **In this chapter** we explore the murkiness that can suddenly manifest itself when the mantle of the expert topic is potentially frightening or embarrassing. These types of topics may have been chosen by the students or suggested by teachers who feel such topics ought to be handled through drama but then worry about setting them up safely and productively.

The three scenarios in the title of this chapter reflect actual themes chosen by students at different times in our teaching experience. Of all the ways of guaranteeing the necessary "distancing" for the students, a mantle of the expert approach has the greatest potential for solid learning from such topics.

It is arguable, of course, whether drama can ever be dangerous. Some say that drama, by its very nature, is always at one remove and that this is its built-in safety factor. They contend that a young person using drama is operating within the "safety" of make-believe, that drama becomes a healthy repository for all kinds of illegal, immoral, or destructive behaviors. On the other hand, it seems a very thin line between a role continually assumed in the alleged fiction of make-believe and a role practiced by one's real-life personality: an adolescent who constantly seizes the opportunity to play the role of a sadist in drama class may be shaping his personality in that direction as much as the youth who looks for sadistic opportunities in real life.

There is no doubt that performed drama continually invites actors to identify with characters under stress. Professional actors learn to develop a "self-spectator" to trigger a warning when the line between character and self is in danger of disappearing. But this kind of long-term identification over a period devoted to intensive rehearsal and performance is rarely relevant to the school classroom. Indeed the problem for our classroom drama is more likely to be the *lack* of identification: that the temporary brush with a character's stress is of such a superficial kind that no worthwhile identification takes place. (Gavin has painful memories of "dying of the plague" becoming a laugh a minute!)

Nevertheless, there is, we believe, a real danger—that of *manipulation.* It may well be that the adolescent mentioned above is perfectly in control of himself in playing a sadistic role as part of classroom drama, but are the other participants, those at the receiving end of his "fictitious" sadism, equally in control of themselves, or have they been trapped into an unpleasant drama they were not ready for? This "readiness" is pertinent, for if they had known what they were getting into their defenses would have been alerted. It may seem, then, that the notion of drama as a safe repository for all kinds of antisocial behaviors is too facile an explanation in that it fails to take other members of the group into account: one student's therapeutic indulgence may overstep the threshold of another's vulnerability.

And what about the power of the teacher? Can she too manipulate her students into a level of identification with stress that they are not ready for? When a group of students invest their trusting, serious, committed selves into a delicate topic, the teacher, with the best of intentions, may leave those young people unprotected. The teacher may be so delighted at having a class prepared to work seriously on a serious topic that she plunges them into stressful characterization without realizing that she needs to structure some "protection" at each stage of the work. It is not necessarily the *topic* that is at fault (although it may conceivably be inappropriate for a particular group or at a particular time); it is the *treatment* that can be dangerous. We cannot think of a subject that cannot or should not be tackled through drama. But we also suggest that *circumstances,* personal, professional, legal, or political, may emphatically exclude certain topics—if you had a phobia about teddy bears or taught in a country where teddy bears were banned, you might be wise to avoid the subject of teddy bears!

If you are the kind of teacher who assumes that whatever the topic, it should be entered through "characterization," then you take the risk that your students, in their attempt to express the pain felt by those fictional characters, will retreat into glibness or expose themselves to distress. Of course, you may be a wise, experienced teacher who knows your students well and also knows how to protect them "into" (as opposed to protecting them "from") becoming those characters. In that case, the drama will be a rich learning experience.

The mantle of the expert approach precludes the risk of glibness or distress by offering an alternative starting point to characterization. In this chapter, we discuss some of the conventions that serve to "protect," using three topics suggested, at various times, by Dorothy's classes:

1. Watergate. (These lessons took place in 1976.)
2. Crying When Someone Dies.
3. Cancer: Finding a Cure (These lessons took place during the final days before President Nixon resigned.)

In each case, the students were under ten years old (the children who chose "death" were only seven, the "cancer" class were barely more than that). They were also attending summer classes, so they were there voluntarily or had been enrolled by their parents.

We will give a broad description of each of the three sequences of lessons and use the material to illustrate our argument about protection. (For a full, detailed account of one of Dorothy's mantle of the expert segments, see Chapter 8, *King Arthur.*)

Dorothy's first concern in each case was what the topic *meant* to the students. "Watergate" was suggested in the context of making a national museum to celebrate America's bicentennial year. Other sections of the museum were to be created to explain the Mechlenburg Declaration of Independence; the freeing of the slaves by Abraham Lincoln; the flight of the Wright brothers; and the Declaration of Independence signed by Mr. Jefferson and his contemporaries. "Death," the second example, was mentioned in discussing why people cry—someone started crying in class as a result of an accident while playing just before the session started. "Cancer," the third example, was one of a range of subjects raised in answer to a question about "the biggest problems facing the world."

Thus in each case there was a rational cause prompting the ideas to merge: the first was triggered by students' telling Dorothy about the bicentennial celebrations to be held in Winston–Salem, North Carolina; the second by someone's crying, and the third by the teacher's question. These then were translated into "safe" contexts: (1) designing a museum to help people understand Watergate and other events in our history; (2) creating the "best comforting room in the world" as part of running a wondrously sympathetic funeral home; and (3) trying (but not succeeding) as scientists to find a cure for cancer.

These contexts must seem curious to teachers whose instinct is to "go for the action." There is an understandable but, we believe, overrated belief that drama is about reexperiencing the *thrill* of an actual or fictional experience. Dorothy chose these contexts with a view to:

- Protecting the students within the dramatic event.
- Protecting them within the social event (i.e., among their peers).
- Enabling them to penetrate the surface action of an event in order to bring about some new perception.
- Using the event to learn something related to the school curriculum.
- Setting up the "power to influence" within the tasks demanded by the "enterprise."

Watergate

The emphasis here had to be on "running a museum," Watergate being but one part of the enterprise. It had to be a *wax* museum, so that one of the principal tasks would be to devise tableaux illustrating different aspects of the Watergate events, aspects revealing both *facts* and *feelings*. The rationale went as follows:

> We, the museum curators, will need to give the wax-model makers instructions for the tableaux. Can we temporarily use our physical selves (shuffling ourselves around like chessmen) to "stand in" for the models as a way of being absolutely certain what it is we want these models to teach the public? People have to understand that what went on at the time of Watergate was very complex. And oh, yes, we must give instructions about the feelings the models will have to portray. We'll pin lines of dialogue—say between Mr. and Mrs. Nixon—on our shoulders, with *their private thoughts,* which they don't tell each other, underneath. The model makers should get the right idea from that.

Thus: "President Nixon *said:* 'Are we having dinner at home?' but he *thought:* 'I wonder how long this can go on?'" "Mrs. Nixon *said:* 'I let the cook leave early but it's all ready,' while she *thought:* 'I think Richard must have been mad.'" The students incorporated two properties; a standard lamp near Mr. Nixon and a statue (represented by another child) of a child in bronze at the back of the room.

Nixon's visits to Russia were represented by a model standing beside a globe of the world with one hand on Russia and the other pointing forward. The card read: "President Nixon *said:* 'I did something about the Cold War' and *thought:* 'They'd better remember *that* when they write me into the history books.'"

Whenever possible, Dorothy makes adult resource materials available—books, journals, maps, paintings, etc. For this topic there was a transcript of the judicial proceedings that led to Nixon's expulsion from Presidency. How does one get young children to begin to access this formidable tome, metaphorically out of their reach?

Typically, Dorothy uses theatrical devices to make books like this at first seem *in actuality* "out of reach." She placed the book prominently on a well-positioned table designated the "library," to be approached only through her as the "librarian" *who held the (imaginary) key* to the bookcase in which this rare book was kept. A child had to follow the formalities of getting permission from the librarian and waiting for the key to be produced and the lock turned. When a student succeeded in surmounting these procedural obstacles, any barriers to understanding the information *in* the book itself seemed, by comparison, not insurmountable, especially since Dorothy had slipped in bookmarks labeled "Howard Hunt," "Gordon Liddy," "H. R. Haldeman," and "John D. Ehrlichman." The volume was too unmanageable for anything more than selective "dipping into," but as the students gained confidence, they browsed unaided.

What began as a general condemnation of Mr. Nixon by the students changed through the making of the tableaux to a more discriminating understanding, because getting the picture to tell the story slowed down the pace of the telling considerably, *allowing time for implications to emerge.* For example, in the portrait of McCord and Liddy, the two men (and their police guards) were in separate "cells" close enough to call to each other. They were depicted as preparing their cases—Liddy, as a lawyer, devising his own defense, McCord consulting with a lawyer. The crumpled-up, discarded pieces of paper outside their respective cells, when opened, were found to contradict each other—one of the inevitable repercussions, the students began to realize, of a political act kept secret.

Crying When Someone Dies

The rationale here was: "Making a special place for sad people as comfortable as possible." The students, in their role as funeral directors and wreath designers, spent a lot of time considering burial clothes and flower arrangements suitable for specific circumstances. For example, for Colonel Johnson, 64, who had lost a leg in Vietnam, they arranged for a full-dress uniform (with *two* boots!) created a war tank out of carnations, and designed bouquets that looked like medals.

All the initial "cases" were elderly people, as was seemly for a young class. They ventured into pets at a later stage because it was felt that the loss of pets also makes people cry. Their "crying handkerchieves" were of the finest linen. Their casket handles (note this singling out of an exterior element of the casket, not the casket itself) were beautiful *and* functional: in mantle of the expert, they have to be designed to really work, be easy to hold, have no sharp edges, be made of metal appropriate for the required strength and appearance, be cost effective, be available to poor as well as rich people.

This protective "busyness" of making sure everything runs smoothly is a "mirror" like the one Tennyson's Lady of Shallott looks through in order to see life beyond: preparing handles for caskets summons images of people having to be carried; designing motifs on handkerchiefs takes them into the lives of the mourners or of the person they are mourning. Whatever they are "busy" with—picking music to create the right mood, getting the procession paced out right, writing an obituary to be printed in the local paper, arranging accommodations for visiting relatives, designing a "cool room" for bouquets, maintaining a garden and an aviary; painting a picture of what the final service will look like so the mourners will know—provides opportunities for inference. (They also thoughtfully provided "crying cubicles" for the different kinds of criers—the silent weepers, the sniffers, the groaners, and the wailers.) Clearly an energetic, imaginative time was had by all in this drama about death!

Cancer: Finding a Cure

This theme, perhaps the most difficult of the three, arose spontaneously out of a brief class discussion. It is worth stressing how important the wording of the teacher's opening comment is once a topic is chosen by the class. It has to appear to promise an attraction for the students; it must at least hint at a possible first task, one that can be undertaken by the whole mixed-ability class; it must contain the hint of a context, but not one so firmly placed that it cannot be eased into a different orbit (the spaceship metaphor is not inappropriate— you feel you are going out into the unknown!).

In this case Dorothy decided the coolest (that is, least sensational) approach to cancer would be that of scientists, who tend to analyze "things," rather than "people." She began the topic this way: *"They say that scientists who try to find out about what makes people ill get their money from the government in Washington, and the President signs the checks.* [A very brief pause while she makes general eye contact, not stressing any particular student] *If we were going to be scientists, I suppose we'd have to get some money to do* our *work* [She suddenly sees this as an unproductive first step—the work would be focused immediately on 'applying for grants' activities; so she changes her premise] . . . *if we were going to be scientists, we'd need a place to work."* [This connotes "assembling furniture to make a special place," more productive for the young class in front of her.]

But it is worth examining the *whole* of Dorothy's first statement, not just its task orientation: *"They say* [vague, but valuing the choice of topic] *scientists* [introducing the focus/frame, which will be taken up firmly in the next few seconds] *try to find out* [setting the process, not the outcome] *what makes people ill* [the subject of the trying] *get their money* [things like scientists have to be paid for—mantle of the expert is always realistic] *from the government* [scientists in United States are interesting to governments] *in Washington* [the highest level of government] *and the President signs the checks* [the very highest person bestows, authorizes, and *knows* about such projects]. *If we were* [do *you* think it might be interesting?] *going to be* [it's coming nearer] *scientists* [like those important people the President signs checks for], *I suppose* [but am uncertain] *we'd have to* [we'd all be in it together—I'd help] *get some money* [it won't come to us—we'll have to initiate things] *to do our work* [it's going to be all action—and we'd be the scientists] . . . *if we were going to be scientists* [same implications as before] *we'd need* [there's no question, no choice—it's essential (sheer teacher imposition)] *a place* [a change of direction—what images of place?] *to work* [action stations!]."

Of course the teacher does not know for certain that her intention is going to have any of the implications she thinks she's trailing, but she's watching very acutely for signs of growing or receding interest. So Dorothy asked the students what is needed to make a space in which scientists work . . . tables, yes . . . chairs, yes . . . cookers, they'll have to be ordered by phone . . . sign for the cookers, please (an *imaginary* clipboard at this stage—if some of these children who look very young can't write too easily, their expertness becomes discredited as they take their first step. Real paper will emerge, but one sheet and pen for each scientist. Can you see why?)

After moving briefly into what looked more like "playing house," with pans on cookers and somewhat haphazard temperature gauges drawn on their cooker tops, Dorothy picked up a reference from one little group to "red and white corpuscles" in relation to the content of their pan. Gradually a class agreement was reached that inventing a machine to change blood (without hurting and requiring an elaborate arrangement of rollers with gears) seemed a reasonable way for scientists to go about things. These scientists with their clipboards and pens for recording their achievements (spelling and terminology albeit a bit shaky) were of course only too happy to explain the machinery to a lady "who wasn't feeling too well," who left them totally satisfied and confident that the money from Washington was being well spent! Congratulations all round!

However, this drama was "protecting *from*" not "protecting *into.*" And what of *learning?* Dorothy certainly wasn't satisfied, because an inaccurate assumption had been introduced, namely, that scientists always succeed in achieving a satisfactory and speedy result. Nevertheless, Dorothy had to honor their success, so she found herself, at the end of this session, adding her congratulations, and then—after a suitable pause—wondering whether scientists *always* succeeded . . . even when they were in some other part of the world that perhaps lacked the laboratory facilities provided by the American government? A bit reluctantly, one can imagine, the students conceded there might be failure and when asked *where* in the world it might be difficult even for scientists to succeed, they suggested Mount Fujiyama, Vietnam, and Korea. Dorothy chose the first of these, Mount Fujiyama, since she didn't want to risk demonstrating British lack of understanding of American feelings about the two less politically neutral locations.

Dorothy's subsequent plan was to take the students nearer to the topic of dying from disease while preserving a degree of protection. She chose to employ a theatrical convention in which the other teachers of the course prepared, rehearsed, and presented a scene showing a woman guardian (in a long, blue-and-white robe) of three wilting plants (represented by three standing people wrapped in green and yellow—imagine an ear of corn—faces calmly showing, arms enclosed). This scene was presented to the students *as a film* when they arrived the next morning.[1]

1. Obviously this particular convention worked as smoothly as it did because other adults were available to represent the garden. But a garden could still be made without them. (A change in the method changes the learning, of course.) The children could have created a three-dimensional landscape model of the mountain on a tabletop (screwed up paper under a length of material to make contours). Around the mountain ("an eastern mountain," unless the students insist on it being Mount Fujiyama), the children could have come up with their own designs for the plants and the grove. The plants would have to be *not* represented (i.e., imitation plants) but *symbolized* (e.g., fallen "paper" leaves? dried-up "fruits"? labels? Dorothy would then probably have invented a story to introduce the "grove of the dead," taking the children step by step from word to image to representation on the model. Its elements would possibly have looked like this:

   1. *"This is a calm, beautiful grove of trees, a place loved by an old lady. When she felt too tired to work any more, she called all her sons and daughters to her and told them she*

"The President has given his blessing to our Mt. Fujiyama project. The plane's ready. Before we board, you might care to see this film from Fujiyama." In the "film" the guardian, behaving naturalistically, endeavors to bring the wilting plants back to sturdy growth by various means. She grows more anxious as the plants resist her efforts and seem to wilt more. Suddenly she approaches a different place and asks, "May I enter the grove of the dead?" Seated there, in this other place, is a calm still figure wrapped in white, to whom the guardian makes *namasti* (the hands gently joined in touching the forehead while bowing). With serenity the guardian now requests: "Oh, Mother, I have come because I am worried about the plants in the garden. I think they may be sick." She pauses, makes *namasti* again, and rises. "Thank you for listening to me." She walks back to the garden and watches the plants.

We have described the *action* of the film; we can only *convey* its meanings. As you read the words, you picked up resonances, made connections, took your own journey, inevitably influenced by the knowledge that this occurred within the context of cancer and death. The words on this page are but one kind of medium. The journey of these young students was not through the written word but through seeing the action. They too were aware of the cancer context, but without "drama eyes" they would not see beyond the literal; for those who made the connections, however, the scene was a prism that spilled white light into its rainbow colors of meanings.

The "movie" took the *student spectators* into metaphor, but in taking up their own drama again, the *scientists,* equipped with their clipboards (their status symbol of success!) were able to remain solidly in the literal world: they landed on Mount Fujiyama, surveyed the habitat of dying plants, and did all kinds of scientific things to them: moved them into a sunnier place, propped them up, gave them new soil and fertilizer. They may or may not have taken notice of

wished to go and live in the grove. Each day they brought her food. Time passed, and one day she looked so pleased to be in her favorite place that they made a little shelter and planted small trees nearby. Birds and animals liked to play there."

2. The students are invited to make paper figures of this family in the garden. At some point Dorothy asks the class whether they think plants can get sick.

3. She then continues: *"The people in this garden continued for many many years to care for the plants, and when they went into the grove, their children worked in the garden. And so it continued until just this year, when they noticed that the plants in the garden are not so healthy as they were before. They've sent a letter to ask us scientists if we can help."*

4. Dorothy then invites the class to draft the letter that the family have written from their garden, stating the problem. Thus the letter is created by the very people for whom it is intended! They seal it, address it, and when they are at work in their offices, it arrives. It is read, and a decision made.

the growing distress of the guardian: their responsibility was to keep the plants alive—but they watched the plants continue, very very slowly, to die.

Within a few steps of where the scientists were gathered, the slow deterioration in the plants was being mirrored by their guardian: the plants' physical ebbing was matched by the guardian's increasing agitation, from concern to anxiety to distress to despair. Gradually the students began to acknowledge the hitherto unvoiced connection between "plant" and "lady," that the plants' life and the lady's life were integrated in some way. Individual children commented that "the plants were the lady's children" or "she lived for the plants and when *they* died, *she* must" or "she will go to the grove of the dead, but the plants can't." Some children decided to carry the guardian into the grove. It was at this point that one child, a girl, leaned toward the lady and said: "Can you still hear? Look, seeds . . . you didn't know about *seeds* did you?" The same child then stood up and explained to everyone: "They never knew about seeds."

This child brought to the surface her own connections between the plants and the woman; in failing as a scientist, she found a hope larger than herself. The child was working within the metaphor of theatre to bring out complex meanings. Some children no doubt stayed safely with scientists and plants; others, on the edge of a myth to do with a curse, heroes, a wrong expiated in death, and the seeds of prophecy, got close to the human pain of death through cancer. All had been well-protected.

Let's remind ourselves what those protection devices were:

1. Presenting the scene as a movie gave them time to observe, have it replayed, make their decision when to "move in."
2. Dealing with a dying plant is much easier than dealing with a diseased human. Additionally, the *emotional* element, so terrifying in terminal illness, is eliminated from the plant and filtered through the guardian instead; the plants' death is serene and acceptable. The students can control the timing of and the extent to which they engage with the human problem; and those that are "not ready" can just ignore it.
3. Their being scientists allowed them finally to *withdraw* formally from the pain of the event: the President radioed that he needed them back in Washington; their helicopter was waiting.

Thus the students metaphorically waved good-bye to this delicate and stressful subject—except for one child. The "seed" scientist asked if the President would allow her to stay and get more plants to grow. This seven-year-old child exclaimed: "Look, seeds, there's another plant inside here just like the one that's died."

In James Gleik's book *Genius: Richard Feynman and Modern Physics* (New York: Little Brown, 1992) the physicist Richard Feynman, writing about the atom, finds another way to voice the same thought: "Nature uses only the longest threads to weave her patterns, so each small piece of her fabric reveals the organization of the entire tapestry." The teacher who uses the mantle of the expert approach sees the tapestry in the thread and the flower in the seed.

A Couple of Adventure Dramas

■ **In the last chapter** we looked at the problem of highly charged topics. Sometimes a topic chosen by students is difficult to handle not because of its emotional resonance, but because the students simply want to "have fun." This chapter considers how a mantle of the expert approach can adapt to this kind of choice. The first example is an airplane crash and the second is a story about a Coca-Cola Monster.

Canadian Airplane Crash

This sequence of lessons took place in Canada. Dorothy gave the students a choice. Sometimes it seems appropriate to begin by inviting the class to make a play: "What shall we make a play about?" On this occasion they suggested:

> A murder
> An airplane crash
> A fight
> The battle of Hastings
> The Darwin disaster.

These kinds of choices shouldn't surprise us, because drama explores events that disturb the normal tenor of life: when children can choose without any limits imposed by the curriculum, their images are those of exciting events.

Teachers, who aspire to have their drama work affect the way participants think about or understand an event, may find these suggestions daunting; often, they either try to circumvent the idea in some way or precede it with a lead-in story. This is not a problem in

95

mantle of the expert work, because any of the events in the previous list can happen to people who have an enterprise to run—even the Battle of Hastings, if you run a castle for armor makers!

In the work we shall discuss here, the suggestion of an airplane crash was finally selected by a group of thirteen- and fourteen-year-olds (seventh and eighth grades) in northern Alberta. It is interesting because of the way a mantle of the expert approach was able to deal closely with the air disaster without ever involving the students in one. We thought it worthwhile to examine the plot line in some detail to see how the *avoidance* of a crash took the students right into the center of the horror of one. When they said, "Let's choose the airplane crash," Dorothy immediately agreed and, in those seconds while she was agreeing, cast about for a starting point. It was instinct that guided her then. Later, when she thought about it, she realized she was following a sound psychological principle, that the *anticipation* of an event is often more terrifying than actually dealing with the event when it occurs.

Following her instinct, Dorothy preserved this anticipatory aspect all the way through the work. The class developed the following statement of facts on which to base their drama: *"An Air Canada plane carrying a full load of passengers flying from Toronto to Fairbanks crashed at White Horse Pass—and we heard it happen."* That is the plot for the five-day drama, the circumstances of which took the participants into areas of tense anticipation of various kinds.

SITUATION 1

The mantle of expertise we chose called for us to work in a very remote area of North Canada, testing delicate radio and electrical equipment that would be used by oil and mining engineers in Alaska and Alberta. Our promise to our customers was, "If we've tested it you'll know it's all right." The mantle had to be "earned" by learning how to do tests on delicate equipment. We agreed that while we developed our tests, in a compound surrounded by the deep snow of a Canadian midwinter and well stocked with food in case our supply helicopter couldn't fly, we would be the only ones who, through our delicate radios, would hear the threatened plane's last message. The components of the situation are sure to create productive tension, provided time and energies are well focused in setting them up.

The key elements of the scenario were these:

1. *We are vulnerable*—remote, snowbound, relying on a helicopter, a delicate machine.

2. Our work, *listening in to the world,* demands a high degree of concentration.
3. It is a routine day; we are alert to anything unusual *because we are so careful in following routine.*
4. Our establishment is beneath the flight path of regular commercial aircraft, so we hear planes regularly, and *know Air Canada engine noises.*

We established the following details:

1. The testing sequences to be performed—for strength of materials, correct writing, correct instructions.
2. A tape recording of the last words used by the pilot of the crashed aircraft. We ask one of the observing teachers to make it for us, *and* we listen to it the next day before we begin our testing work. Therefore, we know exactly how it will sound when it comes as a freak radio signal. (Please, please remember, *anticipation* never requires trick surprises.) The tape begins as a routine statement: ". . . altitude . . . just leaving white Horse Pass . . . on your left . . . lunch will be served . . . afterward the movie *Chariots of Fire* . . . duty free . . . before we reach Fairbanks . . . passports . . . [*suddenly*] *It's a white out!"*
3. Which machine would pick up the call? A girl volunteered and took the tape recording into her care.

Two things were *not* decided—*when* the call would ring out from the machine and *how* that would affect our routine. So we got on with our work, and the pilot's message came.

SITUATION 2

We next located the position of the crashed plane:

1. We cover a large floor space in white paper.
2. We draw hundreds of trees as we play the final words over and over again.
3. We begin drawing *broken* trees and odd branches and finally, the completely ruined trees by which the body of the aircraft is hidden. (Imagine a trail of trees indicating "bits fell off here.")
4. In our helicopter over the icy landscape, using our "drama eyes," somebody spots the first broken trees and gaps in

the snow. (*The pattern is the same: we know what we'll see; we don't decide when, and in this case who, will make the first sighting.*)

SITUATION 3

We needed to let Air Canada in Toronto know what we'd found:

1. We decide that Air Canada thinks it *has* no plane missing—the plane has made routine contact with the White Horse Airport control tower as it flew over.
2. Dorothy is selected to speak for Air Canada Control and told exactly what she must say and how adamant she must be.
3. We get no assistance. We can, if we wish, forget the whole thing and let "them" realize the truth of our report when the plane doesn't show up in Fairbanks.

SITUATION 4

We decided we couldn't abandon the victims:

1. We fly over as low as we dare.
2. We add further images to the drawing, this time of the aircraft as it lies *under* the trees: the bits of wing, engine parts, the tail and the seats.
3. We indicate people by crosses on the paper, estimating how many people were on the plane. (*The same pattern creates the productive tension: we don't know what we'll find regarding the passengers.*)

SITUATION 5

What next?

1. We keep a twenty-four-hour news watch via our normal radio, which is powerful, until we hear that Air Canada has realized it has a plane missing.
2. We compose a regular world news radio broadcast, each inventing one item.
3. One (prechosen) person will announce Air Canada's report of a missing aircraft (*once again, we know what but not when*).
4. While listening, we continue all our routine test reports on mining and oil equipment. See the situation in your mind. People at desks are working with hands, eyes, pens, paper,

writing reports, holding discussions. Occasionally some quietly listen to the pilot's last tape, trying to fill in the details of the crash. There is an occasional news bulletin spoken by anyone who judges it's about due, and then over the radio comes the Air Canada announcement: "Plane missing . . . all feared lost . . . last report at White Horse Pass Control."

SITUATION 6

Who was on the plane? How many crew members?

1. We agree that we've been given names and seat numbers of the passengers plus the crew's names and duties by Air Canada, in case weather permits us to land.
2. We draw a 737 Air Canada seating plan, identifying galley, flight deck, toilets, and first- and second-class cabins, together with names and seat numbers. (Each one of us invents passengers for seats plus crew member details.)
3. Dorothy finds some plastic bags and envelopes from the college office and overnight at home students place in them the significant hand luggage a named person had beside him or her at the time of the crash. (Some of these things are actual objects; others are just drawn and labeled.)
4. In the morning all the bags are laid on a big table.
5. We each take up a bag we haven't prepared and, using a teacher observer as a secretary (simply because they were there; it did not have to be done this way), dictate a "reading" of that victim's personality, interests, etc.

For example, one bag held:

- A little plastic barrette and comb.
- A half-finished letter ("Dear mother . . . sorry I've not been writing lately. . . .")
- Some diary pages listing hospital appointments in Winnipeg.
- A kidney dialysis appointment card.
- A novel with a bookmark displaying a picture of praying hands.

A boy interpreted this person as being a young secretary just diagnosed with a serious kidney problem. She hadn't told her parents yet. She was flying back to Fairbanks after consulting doctors in Winnipeg. She was concerned about her health, worried about the effect her illness would have on her parents, and was religious or perhaps turning to God in her need.

This was a very quiet session, filled with soft *murmuring* voices, and it followed the same anticipatory pattern. When we were ready, we each spoke publicly of one of the people whose luggage we interpreted, trying to imagine what their last moment might have been like.

SITUATION 7

Adding to the record:

1. We each select a couple of victims that interest us.
2. We write down their "last thoughts" based on the contents of their hand luggage.

For example, one person's "last thoughts" went something like this: "I'll be first out no matter what. Where's the exit? Right. Push. Get out of the way."

When everything was completed—the luggage, the life readings, the last thoughts—we had a sad museum to be browsed through.

SITUATION 8

The aftermath:

1. As we go back to our product testing, we talk of those last moments of the crash.
2. We decide which people interest us enough to speak on their behalf.

In fact we did three kinds of "speaking": we spoke in the "now" of carrying out our tests; we projected our thinking and speaking onto what it must have been like on the plane when "it" happened; and we personalized our projections and spoke as if we were the person who had just died, perhaps remembering or regretting things.

SITUATION 9

The culmination:

1. We decide that what we have learned about the crash is so unique it can be used to prepare cabin staff for crisis management.

2. We set up a full-size cabin interior, with ourselves as robots in separate seats with (paper) seatbelts and our bags of luggage. Pinned on our shoulders are records: name, age, character assessment, life story, and last acts when the crash occurred.
3. We create a test for prospective flight attendants in which they will be brought into the aircraft, invited to serve us drinks, 'read' our personality, and decide how they will respond to us as they service the flight.
4. We work out and test, now as flight attendants, how the flight attendants can activate any robot they wish to hear "what it's like being in a dying plane," and predict their responses. (You can see how the same recurring pattern causes the moments of being in a plane crash to come inexorably closer and closer. We are finally there!)

The sequence of events has been:

1. We test radios—presaging hearing the crash.
2. We hear the crash—presaging finding the location.
3. We find the location—presaging realizing that people are dead.
4. We identify the dead passengers—presaging finding their hand luggage.
5. We find their hand luggage—presaging being able to surmize what kinds of people they were.
6. We surmize the kind of people the dead passengers were—presaging imagining their last moments.
7. We imagine last moments of the crash—allowing us as *robots* to die in a crash to help prepare trainee flight attendants to experience how they might respond.

What was preplanned by the group created the productive tension essential for authentic dramatic experience. *We know it is fiction and by our will we sustain it as truthfully as we may, meeting each experience as we discover it in the doing.*

Saving the World: The Quest for the Coca-Cola Monster

Like most teachers, Dorothy's moments of new understanding about teaching have come when by a happy chance an element enters a drama that transforms it, as in chemistry. She is forced to reflect on how it came to be there and why it affected the drama in quite that way. Such a moment occurred when a group of seven- and eight-year-olds came to Fairview College in Alberta, Canada, to work for ten afternoons.

In the course of the work two science components became possible: how liquids can change color and volume when heated and the main organs of the human body. These just emerged quite suddenly in addition to all the other possibilities which were predictable from the way the work began.

The students in first and second grades chose to be *triple A spies.* The idea sprang from their observing two Coca-cola bottles filled with water that Dorothy had brought with her to drink from. She had sipped a little out of one of them, and the unequal levels led them to suspect that someone may have poisoned one of the bottles. Thus began the quest to find and arrest the "Coca-Cola monster" who was indiscriminately poisoning bottles in stores and bottling plants in places as far apart as Tibet, the Arctic Circle, Hudson Bay, Montreal, and Athens.

When Dorothy reviewed the ten days, she realized that the "triple A spies" had in fact completed an archetypal journey. Archetypal journeys usually have four characteristics: (1) a traveler, who is basically good, (2) is tested, (3) meets adverse and helpful forces, and (4) struggles toward wisdom. It usually takes seven (magical number!) stages.

We will describe the series of lessons using the seven stages as a structure for revealing what the students experienced in their drama. Instead of giving a detailed analysis of teacher techniques as we have done in other chapters, we will simply tell what happened.

Stage 1: Normal existence is threatened and the status quo is disturbed. Our colleague, spy number 14, is dead in Athens. We must go to Athens to discover what happened to our very best spy. It is dangerous, so we must not be discovered as we recover the body for burial.

Stage 2: Adversarial forces put pressure on people, who must accept the changes forced on them. We must pass the test of *(a)* the supreme examiner, whose permission we require to start our quest. We must also manage *(b)* to reprogramme the computer in order to erase references to ourselves and our whereabouts, and *(c)* we must make *secret* wills (in case we cannot return) and entrust them to the examiner. Finally, *(d)* we must disguise ourselves so that our own "triple A spies" unit may disappear. Disorientation is now complete (except that because we are experts, we have agreed to do it to ourselves!).

Stage 3: More and more forces can hurt, and the people are unable to do more than submit and be buffeted by events. We must go inside a Coca-Cola plant; we must carry identification numbers that must *not* be found by the enemies; we must remember *never* to accept a drink of Coca-Cola, not in the hottest climate, not in the bottling plant; we must visit the laboratory and collect Coca-Cola samples without being seen by the guard; we are forced to agree that we will touch nothing and yet we must bring out evidence; we overhear a secret conversation (which may or may not be true) in which the poisoner is said to be living near Paris in a château surrounded by thick woods and which includes a reference to "claws."

We travel secretly to Athens to bring home the body of our dead colleague. We find we must pay the police authorities to arrange a means to ship it back to Canada without anyone realizing who we are and why we are so interested in this "stranger," who is now understood by the authorities to have been a spy.

We next travel to Paris to find the château. We slip inside the gates and discover that the forest is patrolled by a huge sun-bear (a species with a great golden patch on its chest); we see its tracks[1] first, but realize it has a silver claw containing a transmitter. The only hiding place is a flimsy hut near the perimeter fence the bear is trained to patrol. We are found by the bear and have to use one of our number as a decoy.[2] We realize as we run for our lives toward the château that we will have been heard because of the transmittor in the bear's claw.

We meet guards and invent an alibi.[3] We claim we are "agents of

1. Dorothy made two sets of black paper bear tracks, one actual front and rear paw marks, the other the conventionalized American Indian symbol for bear tracks. The students unhesitatingly chose the much more fearsome symbolic marks of the Indians when they examined them laid out on the floor in correct proportion regarding length of stride and angle of placement.

2. A feature of this quest was the amount of playing that was possible. We could keep frightening ourselves, secure in the knowledge we had done the arranging and we were in charge of stopping it when we needed to. The mantle of the expert mindset protected such situations from becoming a giggly game, even though they occurred frequently.

3. Being spies, it is possible for a modicum of professional lying to be used in the interests of survival. Dorothy had trouble with her teacher's conscience over the amount of dissembling, but in discussing the ethics the students assured her it was all right because it might lead to "saving lives."

the boss returning from a big job in the bottling plant in Montreal."
We are now in greatest danger and at our lowest ebb—hungry, ven-
turing right into the enemy's lair.

Nevertheless, we find our way through the château, behaving as
if we are on night guard.

Stage 4: "Power givers" emerge, but usually of a fairly weak kind—
they can be difficult for people to feel certain about. We discover the
laboratory and two lab workers (two observer teachers in role), who
have been drugged by the "poison in the air" and cannot read the
instructions (prepared by Dorothy before this session) from their
boss about changing the levels of liquids by heating and about making liquids change color. In return for food (which we test carefully!)
we assist them and write clearer scientific instructions for future use.
They have a map of the château (which their zombielike state does
not allow them to read), but spies are very good at reading maps!

As we explore further we discover the dead body[4] of our colleague, spy number 14, which we thought had been shipped to Canada. It has been intercepted! We hide the body in a cupboard and
take the key. We go forward into a dark "anatomy room" where the
boss studies human anatomy[5] for his ulterior purposes.(6) We have
to find a way to watch without being seen.

Stage 5: Climaxes of some kind occur and the people are in a hope-
less state. We decide to become "bodies" (statue models) ourselves(!)
and have to be absolutely silent even when the cleaner dusts us with
her feather duster! She also dusts the paper model, and then calls
someone and asks him to bring in more light: she's disturbed the
order of the organs and must get them back into correct order or
she will be punished.

Stage 6: More helpers emerge, but people must be able to recognize,
seize, and use their help. Because people are desperate, they are
usually saved only by their goodness, wisdom, or willing grace at
this stage.

We decide to take the risk, trusting the cleaning lady not to tell.
We help her sort out and label all the organs of the body, replacing

4. It is represented by a human-size cutout. This is a precursor to accepting a "paper"
representation for the anatomy study—Dorothy is testing whether they can get their
"drama eyes" to "see" the body in an adventurous way before they are required to "see"
the body in a more purposeful, analytical way.

5. Here there is a different kind of body laid out—this time comprising layers of paper,
with all the organs accurately shaped and tinted, and removable.

them by trial and error and then teaching her how to do it. In return she guides us to the private rooms of the boss—the very center of the lion's den! Information is given to us in the form of a drawing and a description of the boss. "When you see a chair *like this,* you'll be in his room; when you see a person *like this* you'll be in his presence; he will be feeding his linnets."[6]

We pass two more tests with the cleaner's help—she teaches us how to pass through the room of the dogs (represented by paintings and growling noises made by ourselves) and the salon in which sits the lady "with ears so sharp and eyes so dim." Finally, we arrive outside the room of the linnets.

Stage 7: This combination of desperation, wisdom, labor and ability to seize opportunities turns the tide and the protagonists move toward a new calm time, wiser and more consciously able to shape their future because they have faced the tests and overcome them. The cleaner shows us how to switch on a camera that will tell us what is happening inside the room. We listen and watch Mr. White (the person in role, a teacher observer, has very fair hair and skin and is entirely dressed in white—apart from his black glasses, that is!) He is feeding his linnets with white (paper) chocolate and with a (paper) bottle of white wine beside his chair and speaking on the white (paper) telephone: "Someone has left a body in the outer laboratory. Get rid of it quickly before they see it. See you at 3 A.M. at the broken pediment door. I'm leaving for a while. Things are getting hot around here." We see a very white letter has been delivered to him and he reads aloud from it: ". . . regret to inform you . . . body disappeared . . . unfortunate error . . . spies suspected of being in château . . . will keep you informed." He is enraged and plots to kill us.

We plan an excuse to enter his lair as plumbers, so we'll have wrenches to defend ourselves, if necessary. As we enter (with the cleaner who is afraid but is prepared to help us now), Mr. White activates the electronic locks, so we are locked in with our enemy. We mend his pipes, trying to allay his suspicions while we think of what we can do to take him prisoner. One of us discovers how to open the doors and we surround him and accuse him (it was amazing to see and hear a seven-year-old child speaking like a Cassandra,

6. Dorothy introduced linnets because the evil one should, in a mythic quest, be more than just a "bad person." Birds were easier to represent than cats or dogs or snakes because they could be in cages, and they enabled Mr. White to have a domestic personal existence. He loved his birds and though he did sometimes give them white chocolate, he sometimes let them fly about the room and their cage was very large—six feet by four feet (a layered drawing on a wall, the same convention used for the anatomy body).

filling the room with the power of this valedictory statement): "You will be accused in court and on our evidence found guilty of endangering children."

So, Mr. White is our prisoner; the status quo is restored and we are wiser and stronger.

This is a unique mantle of the expert experience in that all the tasks can be performed in the expressive dramatic mode—in the action of existential playing—because spies must always behave in contact with those who must be spied on and always face the immediate danger of discovery. It therefore breaks a rule basic to all the other models we have discussed: that the experts must never be asked actually to manufacture what they make (spies, of course, make danger, not objects, but the principle is the same).

A typical mantle of the expert approach would be to have the participants "run a school for spies," but Dorothy relinquished this for a more direct approach, because she thought these relatively young students deserved their "fearsome adventure."

Indeed this particular drama brought Dorothy and the class very close to a typical adventure drama—a simulation—except that Dorothy preserved two other basic laws of mantle of the expert: *point of view* and *episode*. During the early stages of this work, Dorothy realized the children were enjoying the play element and yet were controlling affairs with responsibility as each dangerous situation developed. The spying was always based in specific tasks, but being performed by spies (triple A calibre!), they were always undertaken with the self-spectator naturally awake. It was this that was regulating the group behavior. Dorothy's discussion before and after each episode directed the students' attention to judging whether any character they met on their journey was a "power taker" or "power giver" (concepts also basic to myth). The distinctions were clear in the early stages, but the cleaner was the turning point: *"We can have a person in the next room who may be a taker or she may be a giver. Can you risk your judgment? If so, look into the next room."*

From an early stage of the drama on, the students were invited to preselect a dimension of the adventure and anticipate the implications of their selection. Each episode was a kind of test of "them" against the "role" they were to meet (usually, with the exception of Mr. White and the zombies, played by Dorothy).

The large-group cooperation in mantle of the expert work is usually far in advance of that developed in playmaking. In this case it succeeded remarkably well, even during the exciting bear encounter when it could so easily have been lost. And the plot line never took over to hurry the pace.

Here is a sort of hybrid drama—one based entirely on adventure yet functioning at task level exactly within the mantle of the expert format. Simple as it seems, it has transformed Dorothy's thinking: the power-taking and power-giving elements provide a basis for introducing feeling without making demands to "show how you feel." A most valuable by-product is that it provides inexperienced teachers with a way to use drama with another kind of safety net in place— another breakthrough for Dorothy.

7

Teaching Nine-Year-Olds About Another Culture

■ **One of the principles** behind a mantle of the expert approach is the setting up of *(a)* an enterprise, *(b)* a client, and *(c)* a problem. Thinking back over some of the examples in the earlier chapters, we have had "running a museum" (enterprise) for "the public" (client) about "Watergate" (problem); "running a laboratory" (enterprise) for "the government" (client) to "cure cancer" (problem); "radio engineers" investigating for "Air Canada" about an "airplane crash"; "monks" requested by "the bishop" to "write a book of rules"; "running a hotel management training school" for "the Chinese tourist industry" on "how to service tourists visiting China"; and even "spies" protecting "the public" from the "wickedness of Coca-Cola poisoners"!

In each example, there is a body of knowledge or set of skills embedded in the problem that is linked with the school curriculum; the area of expertise chosen determines *how* that knowledge is to come alive for the students. A study of the previous examples will reveal that the teacher tends to establish the enterprise first, before opening up the route to a particular area of learning. For instance, the students become monks *before* they consider the problems relating to the bishop's letter; the radio engineers establish their routines *before* they hear the plane crash. A weakness of Gavin's bullying lesson (see Chapters 1 and 2) was that the students' awareness of the bullying problem coincided with their learning that they were to take on a role as expert advisers to schools—their expertise was never owned before the problem was thrust upon them.

But sometimes the teacher finds that the stimulus for the area of study is so arresting that it would be absurd to try to play it down in order to establish an enterprise first. Let us suppose that the area of study for a semester or even two semesters is "another culture," that the teacher has chosen *India,* and that in order to interest the second- and third-grade students in the subject the teacher has started to read aloud to her class a delightful, appealing novel by Anita Desai called *The Village by the Sea* (London: King Penguin, 1985), which is about change in modern India through the eyes of villagers living on the Bombay coastline. (It is not necessary to have read this novel in order to follow the lesson planning; indeed, we assume you will probably choose a different culture anyway, according to the needs and interests of your own class.)

One way to start a project linked with the novel is to invite your students to create their own fictional Indian (or wherever) village by making a representation or "map" of it using a large sheet or plain-colored curtain large enough for the whole class to sit around when it is fully extended on the classroom floor or on a large table. This moment, literally poised round a blank sheet, is always a pregnant one: for the students, every decision made about the placing of a building or a person will have implications for the kind of village they want it to be; for the teacher, every student decision will feed into how the language, math, science, geography, and art of the curriculum will proceed.

But the students are not in fact starting from nothing, for they will be influenced by *The Village by the Sea.* Indeed the teacher will be noting whether they are able to adapt some of the imagery of the book to the task of creating a new village. It will not be surprising, for instance, if the students' village emerges as a coastal village dependent on fishing. What will be of even more interest to the teacher is whether the students refer to commodities such as rice, chickens, and coconuts, to items such as saris, turbans, sleeping mats, and water pots, to buildings such as a temple, a railway station, or a tin-roofed school, to animals such as dogs, snakes, and buffalos. And are the students able to re-create a village that not only evinces these images but expresses some of the values—economic, religious, and climatic constraints; gender roles; optional education—inherent in Indian village life?

The teacher has acquired, cut out of magazines and newspapers, an abundant collection of pictures of Indian village buildings, including many examples of shops. (The pictures provide an authentic basis for the village. It would be leaving too much to chance for the students to draw what they *imagine* Indian shops might look like.) The students are to select appropriate pictures with which to build a village street, placing them on the sheet and repositioning them as necessary when their placement becomes affected by the location of the beach, the temple, the water well, the school, etc. More subtle

• •

decisions, perhaps to do with where people might congregate, are also invited.

When they are satisfied with their choices, each student is given a small sheet of drawing paper on which to sketch the village plan. (When the sheet is put away at the end of the day, the village is in danger of being reshuffled. Laying the sheet down again later, the students can check the positioning against their own sketches.) A chance is given for the students to rethink some aspect of the village before the teacher draws in the agreed village outline on the sheet. The purpose now is to attach labels (prepared by the class) to the shops and other places, so that the idea of a village as a place where specific functions occur is reinforced. The teacher now asks the students to imagine standing in a selected place—on a corner, in a particular shop, in front of the temple—and to share with a partner "what you can see from where you are standing." The teacher may feel it is useful to do this herself first, as a model: *"I am standing by . . . looking across at . . . hearing . . . peering into . . ."* A few partners may share with everyone what they have just heard in private: "John said he was standing just here and he could see . . ." (all eyes checking on the feasibility of this claim!). "Here" is now (we hope) beginning to become a reality.

But the sheet on the floor becomes both tiresome and too temporary for serious work, so the village "floor plan" is translated to a large sheet of paper to be hung on the wall as a long-term fixture. A group of students are given responsibility for measuring to scale and, with the help of the teacher, transfer the village outline to the paper. The shop shapes can be added proportionately, with the same or new labels added. Now is perhaps the time to look at names of Indian towns and villages on a map and to invent our own Indian-sounding name for our "wall plan." (For our wall plan not for our village—the reason for this distinction will become clear later.)

Now for people. The teacher has cutout figures of an Indian "family" and a long list of Indian names (*not* including characters from the novel). The students select a name for each character the teacher holds up. She then begins to build up a sequence of actions with the class for one or more of the family characters relating to visiting the shops. *"Who shall we have going to the shops this morning? Which shop does she go to first? Might she have a special reason for shopping today? What happens in the shop? Try having the conversation with your partner and find out what the shopkeeper says. Can we hear some of these conversations? Is there one we want to choose?"* As each decision is made the teacher sticks the selected figure onto the wall plan and self-selected students move the character from place to place as suggestions are made.

The stimulus for studying the geography, economy, family budgeting, climate, customs, of a modern Indian village is the lives of these created characters, but it has no doubt dawned on you that this introduction by itself does not stand up as conventional drama nor as mantle of the expert. For it to move into regular drama, the teacher would have to encourage closer identification with "our" shops, "our" temple, even "our" family.

Nor is it yet mantle of the expert, *for there is no enterprise.* And if the geography, economy, environmental problems, etc., are to be given serious, enlightened attention over many weeks or months, that degree of interest and depth of education can only be achieved by the prismatic illumination that a focused expertise can provide. Somehow, the Indian village this teacher and class have created so far must be turned into a *client* for the attention of a group of experts. Instead of students looking directly at a fictional village plan, they need a *frame:* they need to see that plan through filtered, specialist eyes.

The reasons for an outside body's taking interest in the welfare of an Indian village need to emerge for the students before it is suggested that they become such a body. This is where the Anita Desai novel will surely make an impact, for that story is about a community needing help to keep up with modern development. It may therefore seem natural for the students to see their parallel village in a similar light and to suggest that their newly created characters might be victims of a rapidly changing society.

It is when the *need* for outside help is at least incipiently grasped by the students that the teacher can muse over what kinds of outside help might be available. UNESCO might come up as a suggestion, or some charity particular to the United States or Canada. In England it might be Oxford Committee for Famine Relief (OXFAM), a body highly esteemed for its research into third-world problems. Whatever organization is chosen, it should be one that first gives attention to the *study* of the economic/cultural background of the country or region it intends to help. For the sake of simplicity, we will continue to refer to it here as OXFAM.

So "Do you think we could be people who set out really to *study* a village?" might be one way of hooking the students into wanting to be experts. On getting their agreement, the teacher's half of a telephone conversation might run like this: *"Hello . . . yes, this is OXFAM, northern branch . . . India? . . . On the West Coast, near Bombay . . . the village of . . .? Yes, certainly . . . you'll be putting all this in a letter? . . . Yes, we look forward to hearing from you."* Teacher puts the phone down knowing that the first OXFAM step is likely to be the class's composing the letter they are to receive about "a village in India." Meanwhile, she says "Does anyone have the Western India file?" Of course, all they have done so far toward creating the village, including their own sketches, now becomes information about "the client."

The letter the students compose will need to honor their understanding so far and at the same time provide the impetus for many in-depth tasks, such as taking a census of the village (to include occupation, age, gender, etc.) and coming up with ways of classifying this information and information about clothing needs, basic foods, forms of cooking, etc. Again, influenced by the Anita Desai novel, the students are likely to include undernourishment as a problem, which leads to preventative dietary matters and caring for the sick. What plants can and cannot grow in that climate will be of central concern, together with the religious connotations of certain foods.

But of course in mantle of the expert the students' attention is drawn to India *through* the lens of running OXFAM. Thus all the problems to do with being a group of experts who spend a lot of time visiting unfamiliar places and climates have to be dealt with: looking after staff health, for example—vitamins, inoculations, travel pills, advice about drinking water; arrangements for staff to be away from families—booking airline tickets, packing suitable clothing, the cost of phone calls home. The implications for study are enormous, and the teacher and students together have to keep determining priorities in preparation for their visit.

But OXFAM will never arrive! This work is not preparation for an actual meeting between two groups of people, the experts and the villagers. The villagers exist only in the students' minds. The students must never be put in a position of now pretending that they *are* the villagers. They *are experts.* This exactly parallels the way things operate in the real world, where experts *must* identify with their clients for viability and survival. But the teacher wants *her* experts not only to *consider* their clients but actively to *express* their understanding of their clients' point of view (needs, lifestyle, or investment) *as* clients. Drama thus enables individuals to relate their personal understanding to that of the group, but it also (because it is in its *nature* to do this) enables people to be off guard in the no-penalty zone of playing and so to be open to flashes of insight and understanding not so easily available through only thinking about things.

Thus, in mantle of the expert there is rarely a *now.* It is nearly always *this is how it was* or *this is how we anticipate it will be.* The students cannot *be* the villagers, but they can *demonstrate how it was when we met those villagers*—and in order to demonstrate they can stand in for the characters temporarily, as needed.

This does not take the excitement out of the drama. The students will still experience helping the villagers start their banking system or helping the women start small businesses or even the more lurid kinds of helping—to recapture the temple elephant or trap the marauding tiger! We conclude this chapter by taking this last kind of helping and looking at it in some detail.

The Marauding Tiger

A starting point will have to be building the history of the tiger's predatory excursions. This can be done by recalling that "we were asked to participate in a village meeting" at which tiger incidents were recalled (e.g., a woman noticed tracks close to the river when she was washing the family clothes, and then saw the tiger watching her from the bushes; a goat herdsman called out "Tiger! Tiger!" and the whole village dropped everything to rush to the scene) and we were invited to take part in the tiger's capture. The capturing of the tiger can then be recalled within the framework of making a film: "The cameras will need to film how we . . ."

The work starts by marking the wall map with brief notes about significant places (e.g., "the pit [cage or net] was prepared here"; "we waited here"; "the first sighting of the tiger"; "the decoy took her washing here"). Thus the whole adventure is predecided by the class around the map of the village. As we have emphasized in earlier chapters, it is knowing the outcome (presumably that they capture the tiger) but not exactly *how* the final moments of capture will be achieved that both slows down the experience, making it more meaningful, and allows the students existentially to experience the moments of danger. They should also decide how the first sighting is to be communicated to everyone (a bird call? the waving of a white cloth?). Once the plan is visualized *and talked into meaning* during the placing of the notes, it can be put into action . . . the adventure can roll.

If you study the examples throughout this book, you will realize this sequencing is a very important element in giving participants meaningful drama experiences. Group decisions must be made (and *recorded* appropriately) about certain elements that are then non-negotiable once the expressive work begins. Every circumstance varies, so the teacher has to decide which aspects must be agreed on. The social health of the class affects these decisions: if the students require help in cooperating with each other they need to establish more non-negotiable elements in advance of active drama. In the "marauding tiger" event one decision *must* be made in advance— whether the tiger is to escape or be trapped. This enables the students to enter that experience the Chinese refer to as "great time" (we commonly phrase it as "time stood still" or "it was as if it happened in slow motion"). This forms a bedrock element in Dorothy's work, whether she is working in a mantle of the expert enterprise or in play making, alerting as it does the "self-spectator": in "great time" there is the time and the compulsion to watch with heightened perception.

Sometimes an event like the tiger capture is so interesting to the students that they want to do it again! It is possible to do this and still retain the tension, providing a new element is introduced: for instance, the tiger emerges, is suspicious, and returns to the undergrowth, so we have to wait in absolute stillness until he emerges again.

The OXFAM Project Now Begins

The "adventure" described above is but a tiny part of the full project. It is not our intention here to consider the many domains of work that could be carried out in the name of OXFAM serving a needy client, for the purpose of the chapter has been to show how, exceptionally, the decisions about choice of enterprise can be delayed well into the class work. The "real" mantle of the expert work is about to start—but that would take another chapter!

8

King Arthur of England: An Extended Example

■ **This work took place** during a summer-school session in the United States for teachers interested in language development. The teachers were looking for ways to develop their own professional language skills and to consider how this would influence their classroom work related to reading, writing and talk-based situations.

The students Dorothy worked with were a group of thirty boys and girls, volunteers, aged between eight and eleven years (grades 3–6). The course organizer had asked Dorothy to use the legend of King Arthur because a cartoon version had recently been shown on TV, and it was likely that many of the class would have seen it. The course organizer was also attracted by the possibilities the legend presented for using heightened and more selective language. The teaching sessions were held in a college classroom with a fixed blackboard; school tables and chairs were brought in for the children. The teachers enrolled in the session observed the work from one side of the room. The central purpose was to engage the students in situations that would naturally involve them in reading, writing, small-group and public discussions, self-assessment, editing, and publishing.

We have already said that undertaking tasks becomes the means by which mantle of the expert work engages the participants in the zones of learning selected as appropriate by the teacher. Therefore, Dorothy set about finding a vehicle that would reasonably provide tasks involving the King Arthur legend.

People often ask, "How does Dorothy Heathcote *think* when she plans? In what kind of order? What images come to her mind?" The following section will attempt to give some insight into her priorities. We have written portions as though she is thinking aloud; those portions are set in italics.

Planning Priorities

There should be a group of people known for their work involving some speciality and involving work tasks. This work should be sufficiently unusual for them to attract interest from their community. The work, by its nature, should span many generations, so that even the time of the legendary Arthur was not too distant for it to have been known. The workers should work and live in modern America. Some element should be placed in the work that enables the workers to be proud of their achievements. It should somehow seem reasonable for the workers to become engaged with the legend of Arthur of England.

From the above "specifications" she arrives at the following components:[1]

> **First element**: the British Broadcasting Corporation (BBC) is seeking . . .
> **Second element**: a group of experienced beekeepers to agree to work with bees using early methods of rearing, maintaining hives, making honey, and producing mead, within . . .
> **Third element**: the social settings of a community around the period 300–500 A.D.—the time of the Dark Ages. The source of information as to systems of life and bee management will be . . .
> **Fourth element**: an old scroll bearing an account of *Gwalchmai of the Light* as he journeyed from his father's kingdom in the north of Britain to Camelot in the southwest to swear allegiance to King Arthur. (Gwalchmai is one of the earliest named nobles of Arthur's court, written of in the Welsh romance *The Mabinogion*. His two skills were that he was the greatest rider and harpist. He succeeded the great bard Teilesan, having previously rescued him from imprisonment.) Dorothy felt the Gwalchmai story had advantages over the somewhat cliché images of *The Knights of the Round Table,* which is too much concerned with noble deeds and life at court rather than with the real political problem of the times—uniting the whole kingdom against the invading Saxons. She felt that the hazards of Gwalchmai's

---

1. This is only one of many vehicles providing suitable tasks that would mirror the legend *and* would require experts. Other possibilities include: A film company making a new interpretation of the legend. A historical association reinterpreting the events in the light of new archaeological finds. A conference to consider suitable stories for a literature syllabus.

journey came closer to the modern conception of a hero, at least for the age group she was about to teach.

Put simply: A group of American beekeepers, using an old manuscript relating to a knight of Arthur's court as their evidence, will temporarily change their modern management practice to that of an earlier time. They will be monitored by makers of a BBC documentary, who will use this experiment to help them trace the history of beekeeping from earlier records.

Certain things are very important in this scenario:

1. The students will always *think* modern and try to clarify the past using their modern expertise.
2. Beekeeping is a sensible choice because methods basically *cannot* change if honey and mead are to be produced, no matter how great a time span is involved. The tools and methods are hardly changed.
3. The BBC element bestows stature upon the beekeepers; at the same time, in requiring the experts to try out ideas and devise and demonstrate an agreed system of beekeeping in a way that viewers can follow, it puts a positive, disciplined responsibility on their shoulders.
4. The manuscript is a social document (including information on foods, beekeeping, honey making, hospitality, and trade) as it recounts Gwalchmai's journey through the land, carrying the sword of light to Arthur.

Dorothy next begins to translate these elements into *tasks* that fit the curriculum requirement: *People* writing *on a blackboard around the statement* KING ARTHUR, HIGH KING OF BRITAIN *anything they think of when they read that. People* designing *their establishment . . . a place where the public might visit. People* listening *to a story that will have to somehow, later, develop into a written form. People* making/drawing *beehives,* writing *recipes for mead,* designing *bottles and labels. People making a transition from running a business under modern conditions to a time in the past. The BBC presenting the beekeepers with an old manuscript relating to the time of Arthur, or perhaps people discovering it.* Even as she plans these possible actions, she is also recording images that come into her head of what she already knows about the subject—which may not be very much at this stage. Nevertheless, she makes a stab at drawing, listing whatever occurs: Images of modern and old-fashioned beehives . . . images of bees . . .

on combs inside hives . . . swarming on tree boughs . . . beekeepers
. . . ah! wearing mesh hats . . . bees have names: queen, worker,
drone . . . a "bee dance" . . . how they find each other . . . their food
. . . hobby books on beekeeping? Publications by professional beekeepers? It will be necessary to find American textbooks or journals
as resources for the class.[2]

Internal Coherence and External Sequence

The possible activities and the kinds of images belonging to beekeeping need to be woven into a sequence that is going to *(a)* help the
students believe in what they are doing without embarrassment, *(b)*
satisfy the students' sense of logic as they move from one episode
or activity to another, and *(c)* help develop in the students skills and
concepts related to the context of beekeeping and the Dark Ages
and to the curriculum requirements of reading, writing, and talking.
All these strands combine to give the students a coherent experience,
what might be called internal, coherence, *internal because what is
happening to the students does not necessarily show.* But there is another way of describing the work—by giving an account of the activities as a more casual observer might see them, as a series of
episodes. These *external* features may not make logical sense to an
observer. It is the logic of the inner development that has to make
sense, and unskilled onlookers may not always see this.

For many drama teachers and their students the conception of
sequencing is frequently related to story line; therefore, they often
find it difficult to envisage the notion of internal coherence and expect the external features to make a good story. This expectation is
in part due to the long-held tradition of "getting something ready for
an audience," which includes clarity of story line.

Now there *is* a form of spectatorship that is vital to all Dorothy's
work, especially her mantle of the expert approach. This is *the spectator in the head.* It is worth looking at this notion in some detail
before proceeding with our lesson analysis. It consists of three elements:

1. Pressure from the fiction. The teacher encourages the
    realization that "our work is always subject to
    examination"—there is always built into the fiction the

---

2. Some of the best materials to use in school are old "guides" and magazines of the 1930s,
because they usually have simple line illustrations of tools and direct instructions on
making and using.

need to have the work viewed by someone else (e.g.,
teaching others about the work or explaining the work to
each other as part of their fictitious roles).
2. Pressure from setting one's own standards. The students
must always be conscious that it is *their* skills and effort
that are sustaining the fiction—the habit of self-monitoring
must be inculcated.
3. Enjoying watching oneself creating fiction. The fiction
must never become true for the participants in the real-life
sense, but it must be *truthful*—the spectator in the head
guards against confusion.

But to get back to our example. What follows is a considerably
detailed step-by-step account of the ten three-hour sessions on King
Arthur. Each session consists of several episodes, each episode building on the preceding one. The record of each episode consists of an
opening description of the *external activity,* which any casual observer of Dorothy's teaching would recognize. Following this external description, we analyze and comment on Dorothy's objectives for
the episode, bringing out the internal coherence, which is more difficult to observe. But first, here is story that will be "discovered" by
the BBC. (See Appendix D for the Pronounciation guide.)

The Tale of the Oath Swearing of Gwalchmai, Son of Lot of Orcade, to Arthur, Emperor of the Britains

I rode the Roman road toward the Bernician border, riding at a
trot upon my noble Ceincaled, and met no one all the day.
Toward evening it began to rain. When I saw the camp below
me, it was a grand and welcome sight. The fires burned red
bright against the slate colour of the bare hills. In the dim light I
could see the picket lines. There were men singing, hot food,
and strong, sweet mead, the honey wine.
   I left Ceincaled, rubbed down and munching grain at the
picket lines, and limped to the main fire. The warriors greeted
me and gave me a horn of mead and barley bread still hot from
baking on the stones.
   Then the sound of a harp broke the silence. Teilesan smiled
at me, then bent to his song: high, pure notes like a silver
thread across the air. Arthur rose when the music stilled and
beckoned me to his tent, bidding me be seated. He caught up a
horn of mead and offered it to me, taking up another for
himself. Then he came and stood beside me saying, "Gwalchmai,
who saved Teilesan, rider of Ceincaled, the horse no other

warrior can ride, there is work here for you; the Companions and I would be very glad of you."

I knelt before him and said, "Since you fight for the Light, how could I wish for more?" and I kissed the great ring he wore upon his finger. Then Arthur led me from his tent to where the Companions stood beside Ceincaled, who neighed at my approach and bent his head to mine. "You shall be our witnesses," said Arthur to Bedwyr, Cei, and Agravaine. "Call the rest and we will swear the oaths now."

The wind set the clouds scudding across the dark sky and whispered against the bare branches of a mighty tree. Arthur stood tall and straight, the wind lifting his purple cloak. I dropped to one knee and Agravaine, Bedwyr, and Cei stepped to Arthur to be close to hear the oath. Then I drew from his scabbard the sword Caledvwlch and swore the oath, which Teilesan led me through word by word, the oath that all now know: *"I Gwalchmai, son of Lot of Orcade, do now swear to follow the Lord Arthur, Emperor of Britains, Dragon of the Island; to fight at his will against all his enemies, to hold with him and obey him at all times and places. My sword is his sword until death. This I swear in the name of Father, Son, and Spirit, and if I fail of my oath may the earth open and swallow me, the sky break and fall on me, the sea rise and drown me. So be it."*

Arthur reached out his hand for the sword. The radiance lit it, growing greater and whiter until it seemed that Arthur held a star. And Arthur spoke: "I swear to use this sword, of Light, in Light, to work Light, upon this realm, so help me God."

The great radiance slowly faded from the sword as Arthur gave it back into my keeping. I stood, sheathing Caledvwlch, sword of the Light.

"Witnessed," spoke Teilesan. "Witnessed," said Arthur, Agravaine, Cei, and Bedwyr, and all the Companions murmured their agreement, as the wind stilled in the great tree.

Day 1, Episode 1

EXTERNAL ACTIVITY

The class members gather at the blackboard to discuss anything that occurs to them when they read the statement: KING ARTHUR, HIGH KING OF BRITAIN. Some students write down their thoughts.

INTERNAL COHERENCE

Language skills: talk; write; listen; read.
Frame (students): simply a group of students, examining a statement; not in role.

Frame (teacher): simply a nonjudgmental teacher, assisting; not in role.

Materials: blackboard; chalk.

Preparation: write KING ARTHUR, HIGH KING OF BRITAIN on the blackboard and draw symbols, such as crown and sword, before class.

Strategies: sit among the students; focus on the statement, *not* on Dorothy or each other; use a musing tone; make connections between students' contributions and implications of the text.

Explicit Purpose (imposed by teacher): to make King Arthur central in some way.

Purpose for inner coherence:

1. To ease the class into being comfortable in the presence of the observing teachers, each other, and Dorothy.
2. To arouse interest in the possible meanings of the statement.
3. To help them realize they already have knowledge on the subject.
4. To empower them to use the blackboard and write down their ideas on it.
5. To help them begin to realize the *areas* of knowledge they have.

This first task introduces the beginnings of security, the idea of penetrating a text, becoming familiar with the heightened language, and seeing images related to the title.

Day 1, Episode 2

EXTERNAL ACTIVITY

Dorothy pins the following notice on the bulletin board:

> The British Broadcasting Company is anxious to meet experienced beekeepers who would assist in a living experiment regarding how bees were kept in the Dark Ages at the time when Arthur, High King of Britain, is thought to have reigned and brought peace to the kingdom.
>
> If you are interested, a representative from London will be glad to visit your group in order to explain the experiment in detail.

Write to BBC, Beekeeping Experiment, Bush House, London, England.

INTERNAL COHERENCE

Language skills: talk; write; listen; read.
Frame (students and teacher): no change.
Materials: a large piece of paper containing the BBC's advertisement; an ordinary letter-size copy of the advertisement in an envelope.
Preparation: prepare the copies of the advertisement in advance.
Strategies: introduce new text while maintaining the connection to King Arthur; open students to the implications if they accept the challenge of the letter/text; pass the letter/text over to the class to test their interest. When new material is introduced, it must be negotiated with the class. In the case of this work it was essential that *first* King Arthur and *then* the BBC, together with the beekeeping enterprise, be introduced.
Explicit purpose (imposed by teacher): to make sure that "Bees/Beekeeping" becomes part of students' thinking about King Arthur.
Purpose for inner coherence:

1. To move gradually from talk that suggests "it's interesting" to talk that indicates "this means something to *us*." The teacher's language therefore shifts from them (the BBC) and what *they* want to what might be demanded of *us*.
2. To introduce the notion that we know enough about bees to tackle how they were kept in the Dark Ages—and that what we don't know can be researched.
3. To persuade them gently that it would be "worth a try."

During this second episode the class will gain their first glimmer that the teacher-student relationship is not going to be traditional; they will sense that the teacher somehow wants to "win them over," that this teacher cannot straightforwardly say, "We are going to do a drama about modern beekeepers doing a 'Dark Ages' project for the BBC." She needs their agreement, or rather, an unspoken sign of their willingness to be collaborators.

Day 1, Episode 3

EXTERNAL ACTIVITY

Listing the jobs beekeepers do to get honey.

INTERNAL COHERENCE

Language: talk; write; listen; read.

Frame (students): beginning the shift to "if we."

Frame (teacher): as a teacher guiding, but introducing the "if we" more and more strongly.

Materials: large, "public"-size paper; small sheets of paper; pens.

Strategies: move from making lists in a "browsing" manner to making "if we were beekeeping" statements; say, "I suppose we could find out about bees a long time ago."

Explicit Purpose (imposed by teacher): to list jobs beekeepers do against a background of in-role teacher talk. It is one thing to invite a class to "think about" King Arthur or beekeeping, it is another matter to engage their interest in a personal way. The students, beginning their listing as polite, conforming students (as they did for the King Arthur statement), discover that the teacher's gradual change of language requires them to *become* beekeepers writing a list. This is the first stage of knowledge becoming *owned*. A word of warning to the reader: this "becoming" has nothing to do with "characterization," for the students are not becoming characters; they are merely becoming beekeepers making a list. In other words the *task* defines who they are. But even this may be to overstate their ownership, for the students may be feeling embarrassed at their inadequate knowledge about beekeeping and may actually be resisting the possibility of the task defining their role.

Purpose for internal coherence: In the first episode the teacher invited the students to respond to what was written on the blackboard. Now there is a new element. They now find themselves responding not directly to the teacher, but to a piece of fiction—a letter; a letter requires that they set about listing what they know. Thus the inner journey for the students is a recognition that they are being invited to play a game, to behave as though a letter has really come from the BBC and that they really know about beekeeping. The teacher is in effect saying to them: "I can adapt my language to treat these matters as true—*can you?*"

Day 1, Episode 4

EXTERNAL ACTIVITY

The students compare their list with copied pages from the *Beekeepers Companion* (the information on the pages is sparsely illustrated with line drawings).

INTERNAL COHERENCE

Language: talk; listen; read (compare).
Frame (students): as students.
Frame (teacher): a hybrid role as both helpful teacher and beekeeping commentator: statements like "When I collect a swarm I . . ." slipped in among teacher responses like "There's a page over here that seems to have got neglected."
Materials and Preparation: numerous pages (a few copies of each) spread around the room on large stiff sheets (they are going be much used later) from a beekeeping manual.
Strategies: mainly in the teacher's language and stance, moving between "what I do" and "have you found the same?" "I suppose if we do help the BBC project, these are the sort of things they'll want us to show happening."
Explicit Purpose (imposed by teacher): making a comparison between the students' beekeeping lists and information in the professional manuals.
Purpose for internal coherence: if the students felt uneasy in the previous episode at having to write lists on something they perhaps felt they knew nothing about, they may feel even more threatened at being asked to compare the two lots of information; a moment ago they finished writing their lists "as if" they were beekeepers and now their lack of expertise is being exposed. But a number of things ease them through this awkward phase. The teacher's language is clearly bestriding two worlds simultaneously, and the continual deference shown by the teacher's role to their expertise and the nonjudgmental way she handles any inadequacies in their list serve to neutralise the threat. There is another aspect, however, that this point of their inner journey picks up—the teacher's total respect for and enthusiasm for knowledge, demonstrated by the way she talks about the new information, by the very way she refers to the manuals, by the way she even handles the pages. Thus the teacher is beginning to put a subtle pressure on

them to reach for the same high standard of accuracy of facts and quality of skills and thirst for information.

Day 1, Episode 5

EXTERNAL ACTIVITY

Students and Dorothy go out to look at "our hives" and check honeycombs as if they are beekeepers.

INTERNAL COHERENCE

Language: talk; listen; read *signs,* not words.

Frame (students and teacher): both in role as beekeeping experts, with teacher as a professional colleague.

Materials and Preparation: a little space; some careful rehearsing in teacher's mind of the kind of imagery and references that have been made by the students during the first episodes.

Strategies: it is very important that they hear *their* comments, *their* suggestions, and *their* ideas reformulated by the teacher and brought into the dramatic "now." From talking and looking at things through the written and spoken word, they are now, through signing and talking, going to relate to imaginary things.

Explicit Purpose (imposed by teacher): to establish that "our" enterprise exists. Hitherto the tentative stabs at role-playing have been in the head only; now—and this is a critical change—the students' roles will be occupying space and will involve gesture in order to "sign" or represent beekeeping actions. It requires skill from the teacher to model the kind of actions and responses that bring an imagined object into existence. For instance:

> *Word*: "Let's go and look at the hives down by the big tree shall we?"
> *Action*: moving away, *indicating* opening a door (this is *not* a miming gesture—it is an indication).
> *Word*: "Shut the door, the last one out, please."
> *Action*: edging through door, *indicated* only, walking a little way, and waiting for the others.
> *Word*: "Right, we'll have a look and see if there's any

honey. (*Calling*) Can someone bring a beekeeping hat and protecting net?"
Action: still walking slowly, collecting people, stopping for people to gather, looking critically at the "hive."
Word: "Some of this wood on the corners looks as if the rain might get in—bees hate the damp."
Action: touching hive corners in space.

And so on. Possibly a contract is needed at this point. This would be the first introduction to the notion of "drama eyes," *which must be taught early.*
Purpose for internal coherence: A critical shift occurs here as they move into what Gavin calls "dramatic playing"—being *there.* This is the first time they have had to identify with a *place.* The test for the students is not whether they have the *skill* to carry out gestures and language of the dramatic "now" (they probably guess their teacher will continue to be nonjudgmental, although we have to bear in mind that these students do not necessarily know each other and consequently cannot be sure how judgmental they can be of each other), but whether they have the *courage* to take the plunge. Another feature of their inner journey is emphasized here: they discover that the teacher has honored *their* input and is now legitimizing it into the dramatic action. In other words, ownership is a two-way process. If a teacher hopes that a class will gradually make her initial ideas their own, one way toward achieving this is to make the effort herself to own the ideas of her students. This is perhaps where the earlier ambivalence felt from the teacher's indirect, unauthoritarian yet authoritative approach begins to make some sense for the students, who may also begin to glimpse the possibility of *partnership* in the teacher/student relationship.

Day 1, Episode 6

EXTERNAL ACTIVITY

A meeting is held in front of the BBC notice to consider whether it looks interesting enough to contact the BBC. They decide yes.

INTERNAL COHERENCE

Language: talk; listen; read.

Frame (students and teacher): bee experts who are considering becoming involved in the BBC project; teacher retains colleague stance.

Materials and Preparation: BBC public letter and King Arthur title in prominent position.

Strategies: delay a quick "yes". The teacher must not deceive herself into believing that the discussion about to take place is a "real" one: committed as they are now to the drama game, it would be unlikely that the decision will be "no". Yet it is important that the drama game be played as fully as the students are capable of at this time, so the teacher has to find a way of setting up the discussion so that the pros and cons are fully aired before the "yes" agreement is reached. For the students there will be no break between "viewing the hives" and discussing the BBC letter; Episode 5 overlaps Episode 6.

Explicit Purpose (imposed by teacher): now is the time to decide.

Purpose for internal coherence: having to making a decision within the drama provides an opportunity for recapitulation of their experiences so far, for they cannot have their discussion without bringing the various facets together:

1. A statement on the blackboard—considered.
2. An invitation from an authority—considered.
3. Their own knowledge of beekeeping—collected.
4. New information about beekeeping—compared and recorded.
5. Their own enterprise—beginning to come alive by creating a place and objects.
6. Seeing their own experience in the light of the letter *and* the King Arthur statement.
7. Beginning to understand how this teacher operates.
8. Beginning to understand the meaning of student/teacher negotiation.
9. Beginning to understand what drama demands.
10. Beginning to respect and be interested in the material.

Day 1, Episode 7

EXTERNAL ACTIVITY

Students and Dorothy take a walk around their premises to see "just what we have to offer."

INTERNAL COHERENCE

Language: talk; write; listen; read "signs."

Frame (students and teacher): as expert enterprise people, sustained throughout in the context of "our responsibilities to the BBC"; teacher slipping in and out of role as needed, for instance keeping an eye on the students' precision of thought behind their gestures. (During these early sequences when the "drama eyes" are being developed, Dorothy and the class never concentrate on correctly shaping objects by the way the hands are working. Instead, the emphasis is always on the thought and mind image driving the gesture. Dorothy would at this stage encourage word and gesture to be coordinated, almost casually. For example, pointing and bending: "Can you see if I've left my beekeeper's hat and net under there . . . there, under the shelf. *(Taking up what is offered efficiently, shaping net as from long use, quickly putting it on and tucking it in while talking.)* I suppose we'll have to invest in a few new ones for the TV program.")

Materials and Preparation: people and a little space; teacher having picked up new images from previous episode.

Strategies: pressing for detail, both in signing (i.e., miming actions, not mime) and in talk.

Explicit Purpose (imposed by teacher): to establish the beekeeping enterprise more fully in terms of what will be needed for the BBC project.

Purpose for internal coherence: setting a more demanding standard of presenting images, more precise in both talk and sign. Whereas the students' roles have hitherto been broadly is "beekeepers," they now find that there is a process of differentiation going on: individuals or small groups, because of what they have offered, are now becoming defined in terms of their responsibilities: "I'm the one who knows the secrets of making mead." Also being established is the future use of knowledge: "I should think the BBC would find this useful [or helpful or interesting or special]." The whole tenor of the exercise is in terms of expectation; it is not simply beekeepers getting on with their lives, but purposeful selection of what will or will not have relevance for the project.

Day 1, Episode 8

EXTERNAL ACTIVITY

They make an accurately written list of what they think might be of interest to the BBC, including the jobs they do around the compound.

INTERNAL COHERENCE

Language: talk; write; listen; read.
Frame (students and teacher): beekeeping experts, with teacher's role "just a wee bit excited" at the prospect.
Materials and: large paper; pens.
Strategies: bringing paper "from the office"—reinforcing the notion that the beekeeping enterprise exists *as a place*.
Explicit Purpose (imposed by teacher): to set standards of written work, including accuracy of language and spelling where possible.
Purpose for internal coherence: the students may not have expected that entry into dramatic fiction would entail a high standard of written language. It is important that the logic of the need to do this writing, arising out of their promise to the BBC, seems reasonable to them. But the teacher is doing more than setting an exercise in accuracy: the writing gives status to the fiction and is itself a demonstration to the students of how written language and experience are deeply connected. The writing is *personal* in the sense that it has grown naturally from their experiences during the session; it is also *public* in the sense that it can communicate to anybody. There are not many opportunities in school when this combination can occur.

Day 1, Episode 9

EXTERNAL ACTIVITY

They decide to write a letter, inviting a BBC representative to visit. They have to invent a name for the letterhead.

INTERNAL COHERENCE

Language: talk; write; listen; read.

Frame: students as enterprise people; teacher as their secretary, needing help to frame a letter on their behalf; both *virtually* out of role in what Dorothy calls a "shadowy role" in order to give the enterprise a name, but nevertheless testing ideas from their beekeeping perspective.

Materials: large paper for students; notebook for the secretary.

Strategies: the secretary lacks precise understanding!

Explicit Purpose (imposed by teacher): to forward the plot: a letter has been received, and they are now replying, having paused to invent a name for their beekeeping enterprise. (Notice the amount and variety of work that has been engaged in in the space between one bit of plot and the next.) The letter is to invite the representative to visit the enterprise. Theatrically this is the only way to meet the BBC because *(a)* teacher can take on the representative role, *(b)* it is essential the class not take a tedious delaying journey to London (a red herring!), and *(c)* with the class *in situ* all the way through, they can be experts on their own ground.

Purpose for internal coherence: The students should enjoy the feeling of a promise to themselves consolidated by a promise to the BBC. They experience another way of marking their existence by inventing a name for the letterhead. An opportunity arises now for teaching these students about "stance" in letter writing, to distinguish between accepting the BBC's invitation without qualification (weak!) and making the BBC an offer (strength!): "Our position is this, that we could offer you . . . if your representative cares to call."

Summary

In examining the internal coherence of the incremental episodes of the first session, we see that certain factors never changed:

1. The students operated as a group.
2. Nothing threatened their confidence or their competence to deal with tasks.
3. Every task achieved created a product that was logically put to use immediately.

4. The context often appeared to dictate the task, students and teacher becoming collaborators.
5. Information was put to use immediately.

These are the concurrent layers operating at incremental difficulty and complexity through the sequence.

Day 2, Episode 1

EXTERNAL ACTIVITY

The BBC representative (Dorothy in role) has arrived, and is waiting when the workers arrive. She asks to be shown around, and is especially interested in the organization and the placement of the hives. She explains the scope of the BBC program.

INTERNAL COHERENCE

Language: talk; listen.
Frame (students): beekeepers.
Frame (teacher): in role as BBC representative[3], functioning as an inquirer and a giver of information.
Material and Preparation: *copy* of both their own and the BBC letters.
Strategies: asking for details about the beekeeping exercise by someone who is vague on the facts.
Explicit Purpose (imposed by teacher): an exercise in showing respect to a visitor without giving power away.
Purpose for internal coherence: a letter has now become translated into a person who is seen to authenticate both the beekeeping enterprise and the BBC project. This is a new experience for the students; hitherto when they have been in role, their teacher has shared that role, as a colleague or a secretary. Now she is not available to support them directly (of course Dorothy, without their knowing it, will still "protect" them in the way she plays her role); there is now a greater sense of being on their own in running the interview.

---

3. The BBC guest is courteous, unhurried, and precise as to explanations and questions—*which actually implant knowledge*. For instance: "By the way, somebody was telling me that there's a thing called a bee-dance . . . to do with the sun and directions of flowers . . . I think they said . . . I wasn't certain if they were just having me on . . . leading me up the garden path . . . I thought I'd better wait 'till I met you folks . . ."

Day 2, Episode 2

EXTERNAL ACTIVITY

The BBC representative asks whether they would give permission for plans of the whole area to be drawn up and assist in preparing them.

INTERNAL COHERENCE

Language: talk; write; listen; read; draw.
Frame (students): a mixture of being in role as enterprise owner-experts and students out of role needing help with learning how to draw plans.
Frame (teacher): a mixture of interested and intrigued visitor (she can use this role to *give* the students information while appearing to be soliciting it) and straightforwardly as teacher helping them (where necessary) to learn how to draw plans. This kind of mixture will not be clear-cut; one stance will merge imperceptibly into the other and back again.
Materials: large paper for plan; pens; straight edge and measuring rule; notebook for BBC representative.
Strategies: by questioning, actually *giving* information.
Explicit purpose (imposed by teacher): to give the BBC representative as much information as possible.
Purpose for internal coherence: once more the knowledge they have is reformulated through adaptation to the two new elements: they have to see what they know through the eyes of their BBC visitor, who is undoubtedly present to be interacted with; and through the medium of a large plan, which, of course, brings their enterprise as a *place* more strongly into existence. All this engenders a sense that what they have now invented in the way of hives, mead, etc., is no longer negotiable: they have become *facts*. They can only be changed should some agreement outside the drama be arrived at—and it would have to be a pretty impressive reason!

Day 2, Episode 3

EXTERNAL ACTIVITY

A tape recording is made of their discussion about their work, what they think they can offer, and how committed and reliable they are.

INTERNAL COHERENCE

Language: talk; listen.

Frame (students): again a mixture of being in role as enterprise experts and being students who need help with making a tape.

Frame (teacher): as colleague/secretary (in role) who was not around when the BBC representative called and as teacher instructing how to make a sound recording[4].

Materials and Preparation: efficient tape-recorder and a blackboard, with sufficient space for movement between the two.

Strategies: in her "colleague who has been absent role" the teacher can now invite the students to review, refine, and *realise* what happened.

Explicit Purpose (imposed by teacher): they will mail the BBC rep the tape so she can explain their enterprise to her colleagues at Bush House in London.

Purpose for internal coherence: yet another reformulation of their knowledge and another kind of language challenge, this time including their *feelings* about their enterprise, an aspect that the plan does not show.

Day 2, Episode 4

EXTERNAL ACTIVITY

The beekeeping enterprise is embarked upon.

INTERNAL COHERENCE

Language: informal talk; write; listen; read; sign.

Frame (students and teacher): students as experts and teacher in role as secretary,[5] moving rapidly from group to group stimulating dramatic playing by picking up on their input.

Materials and Preparation: space for "free" action.

---

4. The tape-recorder technician can either be teacher, secretary *or* the BBC rep. It promises a link with King Arthur.

5. The secretary is knowledgeable about everything to do with organisation, has a grasp of the web of the enterprise, can assist the "mission-statement" to emerge, may intrude anywhere, but is not skilled at doing the producing work. She needs constant explanations to be given relating to clients, orders etc. She works like oil in an efficient machine, ensuring contracts are made between workers, enabling the flow of energy right through the total business, creating productive tension by foreshadowing, in her innocent way, "how exciting to be on TV . . ." and making the clients add to a kaleidoscope sense of "others we deal with". The teacher-in-the-secretary will help individual children who need special attention—the timid, the truculent, the scape-goat, the show-off and, the loner.

Strategies: teacher observing students' input in order to build
on it, using her neutral, innocent, secretary role.
Explicit Purpose (imposed by teacher): "You're on your
own—run the enterprise."
Purpose for internal coherence: this is the first time these
students have been given chance to "play" (Dorothy calls it
"expressive drama"). It is a diagnostic opportunity for the
teacher to observe to what extent, when freed from teacher
input, they are capable of "living through" in the dramatic
"now," drawing on the knowledge in their heads: do they
reinforce what they have done before? do they invent? do they
risk actions and appropriate language? do they listen to one
another and follow one another's line of invention? do they
start something and stick to it? do they flounder, eyes perhaps
continually in direction of teacher? Dorothy allows this to
continue only in so far as it appears to be productive, knowing
that she has more structured tasks at hand for Episode 5. She
does so without breaking the "playing" mode. Any intervention
by her in her *secretary* role can, of course, deal only with
subgroups—it is not a secretary's place to lecture the whole staff!

Day 2, Episode 5

EXTERNAL ACTIVITY

Dorothy produces from "the office" various items of concern that
require attention:

1. An unpaid bill to a supplier of hives.
2. An estimate from a builder for repairs to a shed roof,
   requesting some details "he forgot when he came to
   measure up last week."
3. A request to consider designing new bottles for mead that
   would suggest a "long tradition."
4. A report of a swarm of bees sighted a few miles away at
   Foster's Farm.
5. A notice that a load of sugar is being delivered next week
   by rail.

INTERNAL COHERENCE

Language: talk; write; listen; read; draw; sign.
Frame (students and teacher): students are experts; the
teacher, in role as secretary, is now creating outside factors.

Materials and Preparation: this is the first time the teacher has prepared material for specific small-group tasks. During this day the beekeeping manual materials will always be at hand for consultation, plus small paper (for quick sketches and notes) and pencils. These bits and pieces are never discarded. The secretary takes them up, leaves notes when necessary, *and* collects everything "before we lock up for the night." It becomes her job not to lose things. Of course the *teacher* needs to peruse these bits of paper carefully after each session to help her plan the next stage, noting as she does such matters as spelling, layout, handwriting, and accuracy of information. The secretary has also taken on responsibility for keeping the plan of the bee-keeping enterprise displayed in her office. She chooses regularly to refer to it, keeping it active when suitable and watching to see if it matters to the class and whether additions and modifications are proposed. *Strategies*: to give out the mail with an air of absolute confidence in each group's expertise, while subtly prepared to bolster any sensed inadequacy in meeting the task. (There will be some loners who choose to work separately. The teacher needs to consider whether, at what stage, *and* using which contextual strategy she will interfere. This will depend on the teacher's reading of why the student is on his or her own.) *Explicit purpose (imposed by teacher)*: to test whether they can think on their feet in response to sudden arrival of new tasks. *Purpose for internal coherence*: new demands are being made on the students here. All their thinking so far has been related to what they have invented about the jobs they do, combined with hypothesizing about what will be relevant to the BBC project. *Now* new tasks have been imposed from the outside, in the form of problems. This both gives a new slant to their responsibilities—as experts they surely *must* have solutions—and a perspective on their enterprise as an on-going concern, which will make demands whether or not they take on the BBC's project. It also gives a sense of *history* to the enterprise, for these letters and telephone calls imply past relationships with the public. And it is a diagnostic opportunity for the teacher, who is noting levels of skill, degrees of interest, level of energy, stamina for details, degrees of cooperation, and attention span. The episode does appear to be taking the class away from the central thrust to do with King Arthur. It is often difficult for the untutored teacher to appreciate that it is only the *surface* of the activity that is moving away. The internal development as described in this paragraph takes the students *nearer* King Arthur.

Day 3, Episode 1

EXTERNAL ACTIVITY

Dorothy is waiting with two BBC responses in envelopes. Response *(a)* asks the beekeepers to help with the project; response *(b)* advises them that the BBC has decided to use an English team of beekeepers. The students choose to open response *(a),* which contains information and details of "a site for the old-fashioned ways of preparing honey, mead, etc." to be demonstrated. It includes the Gwalchmai evidence (as far as it is known) on a tape recording. The students hear the tape. (The teacher can select someone else to do a "bardic voice" or do it herself. Dorothy chose the latter because it had to sound English in pitch, accent, tonality. But she persuaded the class: "We'll all know it's me telling the story, but can we agree that we'll not let that bother us?" It is important, of course, that it is a *taped* voice they are listening to rather than simply watching Dorothy telling the story in front of them—she doesn't want her visual signals to color their images.)

INTERNAL COHERENCE

Language: talk; listen; read.
Frame (students and teacher): experts with their secretary (secretary alternates as teacher where necessary).
Materials and Preparations: two sealed identical envelopes; two letters as previously described, plus photocopies; one outline for a suggested site plan, plus photocopies; one tape-recording with the Gwalchmai story on it, and a machine on which to play it; consideration of how to group the students for this episode so that they will have direct engagement with the tape-recording and photocopies.
Strategies: behaving in two modes: secretary for opening letters, etc., teacher for making contracts and for dropping in the notion that a story can get handed down by word of mouth or by being written—unless it gets lost (remember that the teacher's goal is that the students should study language).
Explicit Purpose (imposed by teacher): to make a choice between two versions of the BBC reply—one letter demands

unwavering commitment; the other provides a chance to opt out. Dorothy is taking a risk here (although all the signs from this class were that they were excited by the first two days), but she feels it has to be taken; she is virtually saying to the group, "Are you prepared to go on with this work? *Now* is your chance to decide." If they had chosen the second version, she would have had to ask them what kind of drama they would like to do instead. When they choose the "commitment," they listen to the telling (in keeping with the oral tradition of which it is a part) of the Gwalchmai story:

I, Gwynhwyfar, wife to Arthur, High King of Britain, put these words upon this waxen tablet, as they were spoken to me by Gwalchmai of the Light, as he lay dying of a head wound taken in battle when fighting alongside the Companions against Aldwulf of the South Saxons. Thanks be to God for bees who yielded up their wax so these words can be remembered:

"I, Gwalchmai, first must give my thanks to these monks here at Meadmoor and for their surgeon who has dressed my wound. I see it in his eyes that I must speak now before the long journey to the other light begins.

"I was born in Orkney at Dunn Fionn, my father's fortress, son of Lot, chieftain of Innis Erc, and of Morgawse, my mother, said by some to be a sorceress, schooled in the ways of darkness, enemy of the light, and sister to Arthur, son of Uther Pendragon.

"With my brothers, Agravaine and Medraut, I grew to the time when my voice broke, and as I was but a poor thrower of spears, I spent much time by the shore playing upon the harp and in the stables with the horses. At that time only Arthur, son of the great Uther Pendragon, used horses in battle, and the Saxons deemed him to be in error. My mother taught me the Latin, to read and write and speak, believing that she could train me to follow darkness and the ways of sorcery, but fearing this, I escaped and had a strange dream as I lay down to rest.

"While seated by the shore, I saw a boat with neither oarsman or steerer launch itself towards my feet, and when I climbed aboard, it turned of its own accord and swiftly carried me to a place which now I know to have been the Islands of the Blessed where neither time nor death nor sorrow holds any sway. There I met Lugh, the Sun Lord, and heard for the first time the bard Teilesan play his harp music. Lugh led me to a cellar, all great blocks of stone around, above and beneath our feet. And in the center lay a sword with a great ruby in the pommel. This glowed red as fire and spilled its light over me.

"Lugh bade me take the sword, and as I lifted it, a great white heat seemed to burn my hand and yet there was neither scar nor bleeding. He said the sword's name was Caledrwlch, which means 'The Hard One.' And he bade me leave and said to me 'Go in Light, my heart, and do not wonder at what happens.' In that moment the walls of the hall dissolved and the Islands of the Blessed faded slowly with the wind and when I woke a hawk was flying in slow circles through the air above me. I remembered my name: Gwalchmai means 'Hawk of May.' The sword was still with me, yet my clothes and shoes were all too small, and when I spoke my voice was settled into deep tones, and I remembered Lugh had told me that a single day spent in the Islands of the Blessed was as three years as time is measured on our earth.

"My time is short so I can tell but little of the journey I made to Camlann, Arthur's fort left broken by the Romans when they departed from these shores and built again by him to house the Companions and their horses. But this I must tell, for when I am dead these things must be done. Bring my great stallion, Ceincaled, Harsh Beauty, and let him see that my life is gone from this earthly shape, then take off his halter and saddle cloth and fasten my sword, Caledrwlch, to his mane and set him free. Let no men try to stop his flight for if they do, his great hooves will batter them to pulp. And do not try to follow him—he is not of this place, and must return whence he came.

"I first rode him when Cerdic, King of the West Saxons, had him in his stables and no man could ride him. Cerdic had captured me and kept me working with his hives (for the first golden mead and honey milk and cakes were made in the monastery at Ydris Witrun) until such time as he dared take my sword from me. Finding me starving in poor garments and without shoes, he thought that I had stolen Caledrwlch from a warrior and he envied the great ruby shining in its hilt. Ceincaled would let no rider sit upon his back, so Cerdic thought that if I tried, at his invitation, the horse would slay me and he could take the sword as lawful tythe for feeding me.

"That ride was as nothing I had ever known before. Ceincaled exploded as I leapt upon his back and we both knew he could not be mastered but would obey his rider out

of love. He leapt the fortress wall and we were free. That
night I knew that Lugh had sent him for that purpose and
that I must return him to the Light. 'Go,' I said, 'return to
your own kingdom,' but he bowed his head and would not
leave. From that day, though I have grown old, fathered a
son, learned to sing the lays of seed time and harvest, my
hair grown grey, Ceincaled is still as tall, unweary after long
days, snow white, with eyes undimmed. Soon he will be free
of my service to wander in the meadow of eternal spring,
until such time as he shall bear another who needs his
strength.

"Sometimes I think we dreamed our lives together, but
then I see my battle scars and know that not all was
dreaming. One dream I do remember though. At the time it
seemed as if I slept. I now know that I have dreamed a
future, of all time still to come, and I pray the dream will
make that time have as good an outcome as my dream had.

"The great Teilesan, prophet, magician, bard, and
Companion, he of the second sight, was taken prisoner in
my dream, carried over the sea to Less Britain and hidden
in a great fortress, one of many of that land. The
Companions and I spent weary days within my dream,
seeking which castle dungeon held him. Playing my harp
and wandering as a minstrel, I sang my way with the
Companions, knowing that if Teilesan could only catch one
cadence of my song, he would return the notes and I and
the companions could seek a way to set him free. Greatly in
despair, dressed as beggars, living off the kindness of poor
peasants, we followed many rumors of a 'tall man, wearing a
fine red woollen cloak,' until one day, oh Joy! our song was
answered tho' the voice was weak and seemed far off. There
is no time to tell you all the dream, but by a clever trick we
breached the fortress (and no blood was shed, no weapon
used, but guile), carrying the bard up from the stinking
chamber into the light and thence by ship to Britain and
Arthur's Camlann. I pray that if in some future time a
minstrel must sing his way into a fortress, it will be as in my
dream. Teilesan, who knows these things says if men do not
submit to darkness it may be so.

"When Ceincaled bore me to Camlann to swear my oath
to Arthur, the High King at first refused me leave to serve
him, believing I was of the darkness like my mother,
Morgawse, his sister. He thought my sword bewitched and
the stallion made in evil darkness by sorcery. Only after I
had worked among the wounded after battle, and tried to
save the life of a poor clansman dying of a spear thrust in

his lung, did he believe my given name, Gwalchmai of the
Light, was true. I swore the threefold oath.

"Many memories I have—of battles shared, the
nervousness before, and prayers, and resting after by fires; of
passing around the golden mead (surely bees are truly sent
by Lugh from the Islands of the Blessed to serve mankind),
the barley bread, the honey and honey milk, while the harp
sang under the fingers of Teilesan—but they must be
remembered in the hearts of those who know me and live to
pass them down to their sons and daughters . . ."

Here Gwalchmai seemed to see a spirit in his room, his
dark eyes flooded with brilliant life. "You" he said, "I am
coming." Beneath my hand I felt his muscle tense; I felt his
heart beat once . . . twice . . . pause . . . the light in his eyes
was dimmed and the candle in the wall sconce went out.
Only the last gleam of a setting sun lit the chamber.

I have done. Gwynhwyfer.

Purpose for internal coherence: as they hear the Gwalchmai
story, they may begin to perceive new implications of
accepting the BBC's assignment. The teacher seems to be
drawing their attention to this being "a story *told*," but they
may also be mystified by the archaic language of the story.
This session may be a big leap for some of the students,
especially those who became absorbed in the quiet busyness
with which the previous session ended—they may have been
hoping to carry on with their group task. No doubt Dorothy
continues to find opportunity even while discussing
Gwalchmai to reinforce what she observed them doing the
day before—"keeping bees alive," as it were, while she paves
the way for a demanding language exercise.

Day 3, Episode 2

EXTERNAL ACTIVITY

The bees need attention. As they work they consider the Gwalchmai
evidence and what changes in practice will be demanded.

INTERNAL COHERENCE

Language: talk (about *both* Gwalchmai and on-going tasks);
write (about their tasks, where necessary); listen to both
"threads"; read (material to do with their own tasks).
Frame (students): experts with a problem to ponder.

Frame (teacher): colleague/teacher, alternating, supporting *both* threads.

Materials and Preparations: people using space.

Strategies: honour the task work started the previous day. Weave into the task orientation an informal opportunity to open up their reaction to the Gwalchmai story (its style as well as its content), and, where appropriate, seize the chance (in preparation for the next episode) of turning the "sound images" from the tape into "visual images." Drop the colleague/secretary role as the teacher function is needed. When it is a matter of the implications for our business, and the students are coping with the ideas at that level, the secretary voice/behavior is best, because it foreshadows "what needs moving to the other work site." However, when it is necessary for more appreciation of why people need to be bothered with old stories and long-ago times, a direct student/teacher discussion may be more efficient. When she is just teacher, she can hold a class discussion on Gwalchmai and its implications for them, reinforcing the notion of oral and written traditions.

Explicit Purpose (imposed by teacher): "The bees need our attention" *and* "We need to talk!"

Purpose for internal coherence: this subtle weaving of two concerns simultaneously is dramatically, psychologically, and educationally resonant. The tug from one orientation highlights the tug from the other orientation. Put another way: there is something about not having time to concentrate on Gwalchmai directly that opens up its significance in a way that is liberating. And what an effective way of helping them to cope *indirectly* with the obscure language of the text! This is a completely new experience for these students to handle; its very ambiguity brings credibility to the whole exercise, yet to anyone casually watching, it might just look messy!

Day 3, Episode 3

EXTERNAL ACTIVITY

They draw what things will look like on the set, "a long time ago in the days of Arthur the King"—their clothing; the landscape; the hives; heating sources; tools; bottles; vessels—and they decide on what kind of place they hope the BBC will give them to work in on location.

. . . .

INTERNAL COHERENCE

Language: talk; write; draw; read images and compare.
Frame (students): moving between bee experts and students.
Frame (teacher): as teacher, enabling the students to create images.
Materials and Preparation: blackboard and chalk *or* large paper *or* smaller, individual sheets. Illustrations of Dark Ages clothing, early beehives, landscape/terrain, homes, vessels, tools, to be displayed *when the students have completed their drawings.* (Later, both the professional illustrations and the students' own drawings will be used as part of a great "discovery.")
Strategies: this is an opportunity to feed images or information while *appearing* to be asking a question. For example, referring, say, to a Saxon brooch in a picture: "They do say they were really good at metal work, but they must have had ways to heat it up—maybe in a dish?" Or, "I wonder if the BBC realize we won't be able to wear any clothes made of nylon and dyed with colors not made with plants? What if they give us Batman red?"
Explicit Purpose (imposed by teacher): "The BBC have sent their version of what they think a typical Dark Ages site would look like. They think we don't know as much as they do; it will need amending and adding to for we've got ideas as well! Are there images that have come into our heads from Gwalchmai that we will want to recommend be included?"
Purpose for internal coherence: drawing is a wonderful way of tapping intuitive notions about anything and the time is ripe to find out (for their own sakes as well as Dorothy's) what the Dark Ages *means* to them, as filtered through the story—not any old images will do. It also creates a readiness to look at more authentic, stylized pictures of the period. Once more the students find themselves *comparing* in order to learn.

Day 4, Episode 1

EXTERNAL ACTIVITY

Dorothy is waiting with the original plan of land/buildings (made on Day 2) laid out on a table. On another table is another "plan," consisting of a stream, some forest, a great oak, a roadway and ford over the stream, and a few strips of land, together with a document from the BBC indicating they need instructions as to what to provide on the site in the way of buildings, hives, tools of King Arthur's times. The students draw this information on the plan with any written instructions they think the BBC require.

INTERNAL COHERENCE

Language: talk; write; listen; read; plan images.

Frame (students and teacher): in a teacher/student relationship purposefully negotiating a time shift.

Materials and Preparation: a "plan" the students have so far only heard referred to—a Dark Ages site, waiting to be completed by the students' ideas and large enough for the students to work on. (Its scale—vastness of landscape features in relation to the smallness of buildings, etc.—leans toward creating a somewhat dangerous place, circa 500 AD! Yet, within it, where the "oak" might be, there is a place where travelers are obliged to rest and a place renowned for some reason—a place where a book might disappear!) Scissors, pens, colored papers, and a silhouette of a great, black, gnarled oak. A brief note from BBC pinned to plan, hoping that the enclosed plan will be a helpful guide and asking for details of the kind of site the beekeepers would like for the program. Cutouts of tools (taken from pictures of Saxon times, plus beekeeper journals) to be pinned on plan (for instance, handles tied to axe heads or fastened with bronze rivets, heather besom brushes and wooden handles shaped from branches, thatched or woven rush beehives.

Strategies: viewing the BBC site; sketching new images, revising yesterday's drawings as they seem to fit the plan; lots of discussion about which images seem right and where they should be placed on the BBC outline; continually seeking concensus.

Purpose (imposed by teacher): to create, using the BBC site outline, the place that will be right for the linking of Dark Ages beekeepers with the Gwalchmai story: a place of safety within an unfriendly landscape. Dorothy impresses on the class that whatever images they finally pin onto the plan will have to be lived with, for they represent the beekeepers program instructions to the BBC. They should also accompany the revised site plan with written statements, suggesting how the place should feel and where the oak should be and what it should look like.

Purpose for internal coherence: to make an iconic Dark Ages, feeding from the bardic telling and the class images; to make a plan feel three-dimensional through talk, so that "we could just walk in there." This is not just a class exercise in sticking little bits of drawings on a larger drawing. The class is required to pick up the fact that something significant is being made—a special place, in a special time, that looks as if it could be entered—and that in a subsequent drama they are going to enter it. The iconic form is not only the most efficient to clarify common thinking, it also gives instant feedback to the individuals who contribute at any stage because of the *built-in* necessity to register it on paper. It allows the teacher to pay attention to the sharing capacity of the class—the way they share ideas, space, and delegation of power to mark the map. The teacher is also listening hard for the concepts that may be emerging, for the language she can support, challenge, and upgrade as she contributes an enlarged vocabulary.

But Dorothy is teaching something more than this, important as it is. For her, history is something that happens *now;* it is *then* summoned *now.* It is critical to her conception of development in internal coherence that the students are fully aware of what they are doing; "making history now" out of "what you can find about then." This is where the metaphor on which this whole drama is based, a metaphor of beekeepers living now in America considering beekeepers of the distant past, succeeds where a drama in which we act at being Dark Ages swains is more likely to fail. Of course the students know they are about to enact scenes from the Dark Ages—but as *modern beekeepers summoning the past into the present* and *in charge of what they are doing.*

Day 4, Episode 2

EXTERNAL ACTIVITY

They rest as portraits (forming tableaux of their beekeeping duties, as though they are the images in the BBC representative's head as she reads their letter) while the BBC rep examines the information and raises questions. The rep then rests as a portrait while they give some of the answers. The rep then introduces the problem of how the saga of Gwalchmai may have been preserved and found.

INTERNAL COHERENCE

Checking the usefulness of what we've created in the plan.

> *Language*: talk; write; listen; read signs; form still pictures (tableaux).
> *Frame (students)*: beekeepers.
> *Frame (teacher)*: BBC rep (with blank cards at the ready for raising questions) or teacher/organizer.
> *Materials and Preparation*: revised BBC plan, as if now in the hands of the rep who has "received it through the mail." Dorothy uses a different table to lay it out on.
> *Strategies*: the scene is of the rep examining and raising queries about the plan (including dealing with inaccuracies). Any such plan will contain inaccuracies and anachronisms that *must* be rectified. If the teacher points out their mistakes, she is simply reverting to a "teacher knows more than you do" frame. So the rules of mantle of the expert approach cause her to invent a sequence that preserves their power to influence while alerting them to the necessity for some rethinking. "Let's try to see the plan with our English BBC person's eyes—he may wonder that we've made our streets straight. And why our houses have upper floors. We know why we've done that, but . . ." In order to carry this out, Dorothy introduces the class to a theatrical convention, based on the assumption that when something arrives in the mail we have a picture in our minds of the sender: the rep is to have a picture of the beekeepers at work as she reads their plan and gets together questions she needs to ask them; they, in turn, are to have an image of the rep at work while they discuss the answer to her queries.
> *Explicit Purpose (imposed by teacher)*: to see our plan as we made it through the mind of another; and to use the tableau theatre convention in order to "listen, even though we weren't there."
> *Purpose for internal coherence*: this is a time for teacher assessment of their product, the revised plan. But Dorothy is using an alienation technique so that their reception of any criticism is filtered through her role and the students'

tableaux. There is to be no face-to-face, student/teacher judging! This will be indirect, subtle, productive. The work must be of a high standard, as the remaining sessions will be based on that plan. The tableaux of their beekeeping expertise *(a)* introduces them to a theatrical discipline not demanded of them so far, *(b)* provides the necessary obliqueness in the method of receiving their teacher's appraisal of their work, *(c)* is a timely reminder of their enterprise, which never must be forgotten, however intrigued they become with Gwalchmai, and *(d)* establishes a sense of power over Dorothy when they are invited to advise her on how she should appear when she becomes the still picture or portrait in their mind and they begin to answer her queries.

Day 4, Episode 3

EXTERNAL ACTIVITY

The new territory is laid out clearly from now on and students start to try out working with the new tools, using activity cards that the BBC rep has left. For example:

Try taking a thatched hive apart.
Use a ladder made of tied wood laths and posts to collect a bee swarm.
Light a fire to keep the mead warm in the jars.
Make some large jars to hold the mead.
Make a rack to hold tools, wooden ladles, and scoops.
Devise a mesh to protect the face when handling bees.

INTERNAL COHERENCE

Solving problems as a way of edging into living in Arthur's time.

Language skills: talk; listen; read; demonstrate actions.
Frame (students and teacher): bee experts most of the time; teacher as their colleague.
Materials and Preparation: cards from BBC rep; the Dark Ages plan with its new additions.
Strategies: invite the students, or rather, the beekeepers to try out the actions that would be necessary to carry out simple-seeming tasks in the Dark Ages. The tasks on the

cards cover many of the aspects of the Gwalchmai story: "Groom tired horse"; "Clean its fine harness"; "Make a bed of bracken for a weary rider"; "Serve broth in a good bowl"; "Place the mead jar to cool in the water so that it is safe"; "Secure a bee swarm from the old oak with a hand-built ladder of rope and boughs of timber."

Explicit Purpose (imposed by teacher): to find out what we know about life in the Dark Ages by trying out their actions and to forge a link between beekeepers in the Dark Ages and a knight traveling in the Dark Ages.

Purpose for internal coherence: having used the iconic mode, we are now moving to a dramatic way of representing, *but* we are not *being* Dark Ages beekeepers; we are modern beekeepers trying out tasks in action. This is the first example within this internal development of this role within a role.

Day 4, Episode 4

EXTERNAL ACTIVITY

Now the old tree is to have its history articulated—fire, flood, children's games, hangings. They consider how the story of Gwalchmai of the Light would get written down. They hear the tape again and decide which part of the saga is to be written by each person. They choose pairs to help each other.

INTERNAL COHERENCE

Language skill: talk; write; listen; read.

Frame (students): primarily themselves; occasionally bardic acolytes.

Frame (teacher): sometimes colleague; occasionally harp-bearer to Teilesan, the bard.

Materials and preparation: the cutout of an ancient tree upon a sky-and-clouds background (see Figure 8-1); some acorns in a bag all laid ready when students arrive; special paper and inks (e.g., silver and gold for doing an initial decorated letter) with which to write saga.

Strategies: introduce the idea that the tree (to become the focus for the Gwalchmai legend) has lived through many important events, ponder "how far back it remembers"; consider uses of an oak tree: shade, shelter, playing, climbing,

the old tree.

FIGURE 8-1. *The Old Tree.*

hiding; consider "what it has seen and heard" (always
bringing the event public, where possible); consider "how it
got hurt." (For example, the students might decide it got hurt
in a storm, in which case Dorothy would invite "storm words
and phrases"—rain drumming, lightning striking through limb
and trunk. The teacher can only build saga from their
suggestions.) As the saga becomes written, the students, as
Teilesan's acolytes, try out the phrases aloud, semi-chanted,
"on the breath," as it were.

Purpose (imposed by teacher): to make a saga like those of ancient times: to see it written; to speak it; to hear it spoken. *Purpose for internal coherence*: to generate complex images of the oak, immovable in a changing time of seasons, battles, births, deaths, animals, etc. Also to see it as a symbol linking our time with that of Gwalchmai's. They also have the experience of hearing their language elevated by Dorothy into a stylized narrative, both in its written and spoken form, what Dorothy calls "sung writing."

Day 5

EXTERNAL ACTIVITY

In their pairs, using italic and regular pens, they make the saga, some taking their work home. They each read a segment.

INTERNAL COHERENCE

The oral story becomes literature.

Language skills: talk; write; listen; read; design "illuminated" first letter of text.
Frame (students and teacher): themselves; teacher as part of writing team.
Materials and Preparation: interesting writing materials, including simple examples of "manuscript," perhaps with an illuminated first letter—it's got to look inviting; the Gwalchmai tape-recording.
Strategies: tempt them to try writing a bit of the story in their own words, working in pairs. Each pair selects a different part of the story, so that by the time the weekend is over, a class story will have been created.
Explicit purpose (imposed by teacher): to translate one tradition, the oral, into another verbal medium, the written. (During this time Dorothy is watching for places to insert their earlier sketches and notes about beekeeping and life in Saxon Britain.)
Purpose for internal coherence: an exacting exercise, demanding hard listening (to the tape) and trying to find the images within themselves before selecting the written form. The teacher hopes this exercise will allow the students to understand that words have the power to change the experience.

The Second Week

We are about to start describing the second week of this work. A strong sense of the work "flowing forward" characterizes the second week, and the method we have so far used of a number of separate headings for each episode no longer seems to match this new dynamism of one activity flowing seamlessly into another. We will therefore change our descriptive style and summarize the external and internal features of the episodes in paragraph form.

Day 6, Episode 1

EXTERNAL ACTIVITY

The story of Gwalchmai (32 pages) is put together in logical order.

INTERNAL COHERENCE

The putting together of *our* manuscript. The students are invited to lay out their sections of the story (some worked on at home over the weekend), both the writing and the "illumination." As this is the first time they have seen the product of one another's work, care is taken by the teacher to make sure they comment with respect. They now tackle the logistic problem of getting the separate papers into the right order.

Day 6, Episode 2

EXTERNAL ACTIVITY

They consider how the manuscript may have been discovered and start to think about how the old tree could have held it hidden for many many years.

INTERNAL COHERENCE

Now that the story is assembled they can enjoy creating a "mystery" of where their manuscript has been hidden over the centuries; they examine their landscape created the previous week, make passing reference to what other places a book might get hidden in, and then turn their attention to the tree. The teacher is promoting the feeling of anticipation in creating a mystery and the sense of their being part of a tradition of literature and history where things can be rediscovered.

Day 6, Episode 3

EXTERNAL ACTIVITY

They try reading their Gwalchmai story in high language, then chanting it as a bard might. They then add information about food, crops, etc., to the story document, based on the information in the beekeeper's manual. These are not in high language but suggest either they've been put in later or put in for the purposes of the BBC simulation of how the manuscript may be found.

INTERNAL COHERENCE

Fitting their written saga together with portions of factual information from the beekeeper's manual allows them to make a coherent visual connection between the two documents. Singing and chanting their written sections *and* the manual information helps the two kinds of knowledge bond together. Preparing the manuscript carefully allows all previous work on keeping bees and the story of Gwalchmai to come together, so that the knowledge of this century and that of the Dark Ages are symbolically represented in the scroll.

Day 6, Episode 4

EXTERNAL ACTIVITY

They agree that Dorothy should "age" the document in some way and wrap it so that their next sight of it will be "as if" it had been newly found. They describe how they imagine it has been affected by time (fire, damp, grease, buried by rock slides) and anticipate that parts they make will be missing. A ceremony of saying good-bye—for the present.

INTERNAL COHERENCE

Having just created the "manuscript" or "book," the students must now prepare the way for "losing" it. Only if they are fully cognizant of what that will involve—for instance, agreeing on how it got into the tree and giving their permission to Dorothy to "age" it—can they fully enjoy its return. Their attempts at reading extracts aloud in high-sounding language or chanting it as a bard might are carried out in the knowledge that they are saying good-bye to "the story they have made." It is this collective agreement to withhold what one knows in order to make fiction that creates the excitement of drama. This accepted "lie" becomes "truthful" as we work logically within it. Such logic may or may not be expressed through action—that is not critical. It is being in the "now," whether active or not, that defines the drama experience. The "lie" is both *limiting* (for when we are inside a fiction we have to suspend any overview we might hold of the total context, including its future) and *liberating* (in that it creates productive tension).

Day 7, Episode 1

EXTERNAL ACTIVITY

Before class, Dorothy has "aged" the document, added "archivists' notes," and hidden it (now rolled up like a scroll) in a handsome box. When the students arrive she invites them to decide whether they want to see the manuscript in its new state before it "disappears." They consider the implications of their choice and decide to delay seeing it. She then invites them to witness her wrapping the box in a cloth and tying it with a rope.

INTERNAL COHERENCE

This "tampering" with students' work (as those who have a conventional view of a teacher's behavior regarding students' work no doubt see it) can be done straightforwardly and technically (simply applying "aging" touches here and there) or creatively, introducing a new element as part of the discovery. In this case Dorothy attaches extra items relating to archivists' notes, *as though the book has been found before and lost again.* Inserting the students' own drawings of life in Saxon times or using authentic illustrations they had seen before, she adds three dimensions:

1. Surprise when they "find" the manuscript later.
2. Corrected ideas, without "assessment." (Their ideas are placed alongside more mature, more accurate illustrations.)
3. A signal that more than one set of hands has been involved with the manuscript and at a different period. (For example, in the margin of the Gwalchmai story, with an arrow pointing to "gave me a horn of mead," an insertion shows both an authentic horn cup and a student's drawing of one *plus* a commentary: "drinking horns seem to have been carried by all travelers; in addition, a certain number of spare horns were kept in

hostelries and monasteries for hospitality purposes. [DH, Archivist, Bristol Offices, 1927]")

Having aged the manuscript (with the evidence of mice, wet and dirt) Dorothy places the 32 sheets in sequence on a long length of sheeting suitably aged with tea/vinegar and fruit stains. *All* the materials are then given a last messing up, judiciously, to point up important words or concepts—as if by chance, of course. The whole length of sheeting is then rolled up like a baby in swaddling clothes, tied with cord, and placed in a wooden box, which, in turn is placed on a stool standing on a silk cloth at one end of the room.

Day 7, Episode 2

EXTERNAL ACTIVITY

Students gather around a gnarled tree shape and are warned: *"We have taken on a huge responsibility to be those who demonstrate how an ancient story may survive fire and flood and be read and understood by modern people."* Four different scenarios are offered so that the students can consider the implications of each in order to select *one.* They choose "the bull's horn."

INTERNAL COHERENCE

Dorothy now moves the box in front of an even larger "old oak" silhouette, the two plans (of the modern American site and of the ancient Dark Ages site) on either side. She reminds them of their roles: *"You know, when I went to bed last night I kept seeing the manuscript lying lost in the old tree and I couldn't help but think we've taken a very big job on with the BBC—helping people who see the program to understand life for travelers in the time of King Arthur. I get a bit nervous when I think about it."* She now offers them a selection of four scenarios in which the manuscript can be found, using a paper cutout to represent each one:

    A swarm of bees (tan-colored).
    A child's school cap (white with a green shade).
    A bull's horn (gray, black, and white).
    A lightning shaft (a silver zig-zag).

Each action receives equal status—*they* must decide, not the teacher. They chose the "bull's horn."

Day 7, Episode 3

EXTERNAL ACTIVITY

They break down the finding into its stages and agree there will be
ten moments of high drama. The bull's horn symbol is now placed
in a branch of the tree (tree is on a large table); the trunk of the tree
is "split" (with scissors).

INTERNAL COHERENCE

This is a "blackboard" episode, *planning* the stages of our "bull"
incident, each stage based on suggestions from the students:

> "The time when we were at work on a normal day."
> "The time when we realized the storm was violent and
> dangerous and closed the windows."
> "The time when we first heard the bull bellow."
> "The time when we went out in the storm and *saw,* in the
> distance, the bull caught!"
> "The time when we began to run . . . and we realized the bull
> was trapped and in pain."
> "The time when we saw his poor torn horn and his agony. We
> felt so helpless. His pain made him so powerful."
> "The time when we sent John back for ropes and a
> hypodermic, and waited."
> "The time when we managed to quiet him and fasten the rope
> to a great branch."
> "The time when the split trunk revealed the box to our gaze."

The above ten statements may suggest to the reader that we are in
for a long session, but they represent *moments* rather than stages.
Notice that the statements are all concerned with *actions,* not feelings
or reasons. This is the key to how the experience is to be set up.
Many teachers would expect they should at this point let their class
do a reenactment of the event, with the young actors "emoting" the
crisis. Experienced drama teachers will recognize that such an attempt at simulating a dramatic incident usually takes the participants
away from truthfulness. In real life any crisis is made up of people's
actions, inactions, and feelings of stress. Again, in real life, when the
crisis is over, you can describe to someone else either what you did
or how you felt or both. The method Dorothy employed on this

occasion was to use a theatre form that would take away from the students the responsibility of showing emotion.

Day 7, Episode 4

EXTERNAL ACTIVITY

Dorothy gives them a dramatic format by which to experience their plan *and* record their experiences "for the benefit of the watchers of the program on bees."

INTERNAL ACTION

They could *do* things or *see* things. Thus, hearing Dorothy pronounce the first step of their own plan dramatically: "There was the time when we were at work on a normal day," they could treat it as an invitation to engage in demonstrative actions for a few moments, enough to establish the setting (by "enough" we mean absolute *minimum*). They hear Dorothy's voice break in: "The time came when we realized there was a storm . . . a violent and dangerous one." (Notice that Dorothy is being true to *their* words, planned on the blackboard; this is *the text*.) This invitation is more open; those who wish can go and shut windows or seek to protect something they are using, or they can stare out of the window at the storm. Because the center of the action is going to be focused on "the bull caught in their tree," in other words *outside* themselves, there is going to be a lot of staring. Dorothy has given them a convention for this: *binoculars,* that is, a representation of binoculars, made by curling the fingers to one's eyes. It may surprise the reader how effective this can be in giving significance to what is seen—from near to far, from wide to narrow, all is to be *focused.* This outward sign of concentration activates the imaging in the head, so that each individual can create a vivid picture in his or her mind, a picture *arousing feelings* related to the crisis.

Those feelings are not to be expressed through "acting"; Dorothy has given them another convention—rapid description to an adult listener/scribe. Each student chooses a nearby adult to whom he or she can describe the mental picture of each moment *and* his or her feelings. The adult will scribble down what the student says word for word. Thus feelings are expressed, but through the medium of reporting not acting. Another convention is also used, the sound of the bull's bellowing, created by Dorothy's own voice on tape, not an accurate representation (which no doubt could have been obtained from sound archives), but an elemental expression of animal pain yet undisguisedly coming from the teacher.

Thus each "moment" has a sequence to it:

A statement from blackboard (Dorothy)	significantly spoken
Action span (class)	echoing the statement through brief action or through use of "binoculars"
Pause (Dorothy)	contemplative repeat of statement
Dictating to "scribes" (class)	to tell "how it was"

Finally, a boy is chosen to climb into the tree trunk to retrieve the box. The class, with their binoculars for seeing, instruct him where to put his feet, while he in actuality sits on the floor with eyes closed, matching his climbing actions to their guidance, until he tells them "he is there."

Once there, *they* turn away so they can not see *him* as he unties the rope, giving an account (to which they can only listen) of what he is doing and of what the newly found box looks like. He draws out the length of rope, requiring his colleagues to haul him and the box out of the hole.

It is obvious that the whole of this sequence was contrived. The internal coherence demanded *contracts* about agreed disciplines of behavior, of attitudes, and of image control. It demanded submission to a group plan, but personal responsibility to sustain the landscape.

Day 7, Episode 5

EXTERNAL ACTIVITY

They open the box and unwrap the manuscript, reading it "as if they never saw it before."

INTERNAL COHERENCE

They experience the "fun" of formally opening the parcel, "discovering" the ancient manuscript, and attempting to read bits of it, as if they had never seen it before. The internal coherence still holds, because after the discovery of the manuscript, the students have the revelation of seeing how it has been changed by the "aging" process.

In their minds is a sort of double image, the present new form of their work compared with their memory of how their work looked when first made. It is a magical moment for these students as they search out the parts they had written earlier.

Day 7, Episode 6

EXTERNAL ACTIVITY

They choose, ready for working on in Day 8, a part of the story to "live through" that they think would have been particularly hazardous at the time. They choose the rescuing of Teilesan the bard by Gwalchmai and his friends.

INTERNAL COHERENCE

Using the need to help the BBC program by having part of the story dramatized, Dorothy invites the class to choose a section of the story that appeals to them (having persuaded them that dramatizing does *not* imply doing the whole plot from beginning to end!). They choose Gwalchmai's dream sequence. (The rescue of Teilesan is actually based on Blondel, the lute player, who found where his master, King Richard the Lionheart, was imprisoned by touring Europe playing on his lute outside prisons, but the students were not made aware until their drama was over of this factual basis for the tale.)

Day 8
(This episode takes up the entire session.)

EXTERNAL ACTIVITY

Dorothy offers a dramatic shape so that they will "live through it as it might have been." They create a chamber theatre piece, "The Rescue of Teilesan."

INTERNAL COHERENCE

This process of turning written literature into drama is a very worthwhile learning experience. It seemed appropriate to Dorothy to introduce the class to chamber theatre. Appendix A contains a definition of chamber theatre, the full text of "The Rescue of Teilesan" as it was played by the students on the eighth day, and advice on how to conduct chamber theatre. Dorothy had to write the text quickly, and it no doubt suffered from being rushed, but the students learned a great deal about how the use of stylized language gave significance to this "action" bit of the story.

Day 9
(Again, Day 9 is devoted to a single episode.)

EXTERNAL ACTIVITY

The students examine the "oath-taking text" (see p. 189) that the BBC rep has brought them and together plan how it would/might have taken place: in the forest . . . after the rescue of Teilesan . . . with all the friends around, those of King Arthur and of Gwalchmai. They try it out "for the cameras."

INTERNAL COHERENCE

Having experienced the chamber theatre form the day before, today the students are to engage in an activity that may seem to be regular theatre. But in fact we shall see this is not the case, for the mental set of the students is not going to be "getting a scene ready for an audience" (a rehearsal orientation), but "how can we make sure the cameras are going to pick up the meaning we want them to?" (an experimental, problem-solving orientation).

The BBC rep, impressed with their work on the discovery of the manuscript and yesterday's presentation, wonders whether the bee-keepers could prepare further material to be used as a basis for the program—a demonstration of the oath of Gwalchmai. The rep has the text of the event in a folder, and a large-type version is on the wall for the students to examine, along with an illustrative explanation of how beekeeping methods today and long ago compared. Everything is authentically "signed". For instance, the cover of the rep's folder is entitled "The Dark Ages Programme; Sequence: the Swearing of the Oath of Gwalchmai to Arthur." Inside the folder, the relevant sections of the story line, divided into fourteen sequences, are separated into smaller folders to be handed out arbitrarily to the groups.

The students are invited to divide themselves up into small groups. Each group is then given a folder, each folder containing a different section of the "oath" sequence. Thus each group is to be responsible for preparing a scenario for witnessing the oath taking. The sequence texts include a summary of the external features (e.g., "Gwalchmai leads Ceincaled to the camp") and also the *subtext* of the action ("This sequence must show how Gwalchmai loves and cares for his horse, even though he has a wounded leg . . ."). Thus each group has access to the full story, Dorothy having written a sentence or paragraph regarding an episode extracted from the story, a bare, one-line description of the action within that paragraph, and a suggested subtext.

The sequences are:

1. Gwalchmai leads Ceincaled to camp, rubs him down, and feeds and tethers him. Subtext: This sequence must *show how Gwalchmai loves and cares for his horse even though he has a wounded leg*—everything must show that he *always* does these things *no matter how tired he may be.*

2. Gwalchmai approaches the picket lines. Subtext: The *watchfulness* of the pickets must be shown: looking in all directions, very quiet, hands ready upon weapons, *never tempted to look at the bright fire that will take away their "night eyes."* Gwalchmai must be *quietly watched* as he approaches and *challenged with firm courtesy.*

3. The Companions are gathered around the fire, cooking, eating, pouring mead. Subtext: The events at the fire must show *all are equal, all are friends,* all food and mead is *shared.* There is quiet talk as they prepare the bread, the pieces of meat, and the horns of mead poured from skins.

4. Gwalchmai is welcomed and the food is shared. Subtext: When Gwalchmai is brought forward by a picket someone should take his tethered horse and tie it closer to the fire, and a place be made *as people realize he has a wounded leg that is still painful. They are glad to see him.*

5. Arthur and Teilesan come to the fire and the harp is brought. Subtext: Arthur and Teilesan come to the fire *as great friends, equal in status,* and they are placed around the fire exactly like old friends, either on a traveling stool, a tree stump, or the ground. A soldier brings Teilesan's harp from a "safe place" (i.e., away from the fire—heat!—and from danger—feet!). It should be wrapped carefully and Teilesan should take off the cover and *show how he "appreciates" his harp: its design and color and how it sits easily in his hands from long familiarity.*

6. Teilesan sings his song. Subtext: The sound track will be dubbed onto this sequence. It is necessary to show *how, when Teilesan sings, all is stilled, even the pickets. Only his fingers move upon the harp strings and his eyes seem to look inwards. It is as if a spell is cast*—for instance, meat stopped halfway to mouths—and when the song is over

the *fingers should still the harp strings.* Everyone should be caught in the spell.

7. Arthur beckons to Gwalchmai and both leave the fire. Subtext: Arthur waits, *caught in the spell of the song,* then rises slowly and beckons to Gwalchmai, watching his painful leg as they move away from the fire.

8. The quiet campfire activities continue. Subtext: Slowly the friends continue their meal, *sharing food* with Teilesan, *who gives his harp carefully* to the soldier *after tenderly wrapping it again.*

9. Arthur and Gwalchmai talk in the tent, and Gwalchmai kisses Arthur's ring. Subtext: When Arthur has seated himself and Gwalchmai in the tent, it is necessary that *he looks long and hard at Gwalchmai,* and when he speaks, it is *very clearly with each word very deliberately chosen. Gwalchmai looks at Arthur all the time and looks glad* as he kneels *even though his leg hurts.*

10. Arthur and Gwalchmai return to the fire and all gather around the stallion. Subtext: Arthur and Gwalchmai walk slowly to the fire *so that people realize something very important is happening*—it makes them all rise and move away from the fire and closer to the horse. *The horse should neigh or nicker quietly in the silence as if saying "I must be part of this."*

11. Gwalchmai kneels before the witnesses, draws the sword, and speaks the oath. Subtext: Arthur should be *very grave and very sure* as he names Agravaine, Bedwyr, and Cei to come closer. As others gather around there should be the feeling that *we have all done this before—it must be done in a special way.* The sword must be drawn *very surely* and held high. The sound of the wind in the trees should rise now. The speaking of the oath will be done by Teilesan first in short statements, leading Gwalchmai to say each word correctly. *It is very solemn and the wind should be heard more strongly now.*

12. Arthur takes the sword and speaks his answering oath. Subtext: The sword must be seen by all *to almost blind them. The horse should neigh as this happens to mark the moment.* Arthur should hold it *without wanting to possess it—only to show it is magical.*

13. The sword is returned to its sheath. Subtext: The sword should be *seen to lose its great glow* and Arthur should give

it *back into Gwalchmai's keeping with no envy in his heart.*
It should be sheathed so that *all see it is now safe. The*
wind should still be heard.
14. All voice that they have witnessed the taking of the oath.
Subtext: The "Witnessed" words must be spoken slowly
and *feel very memorable. Everyone must notice the great*
silence as the wind drops.

Another aid for the students is that the few lines of dialogue in the
story are written large on the blackboard, *visually* giving them the
significance they deserve.

Writing all these words on the board may seem like making a lot of
fuss about nothing—after all they are already included in the BBC
rep's script, pinned up for all to see. But it is their *elevation into*
significance that is important—and this will resonate in all the work
that follows. They are *public* promises, spoken as *oaths,* not to be
taken casually, so they must be writ large. This detailed attention to
signing for resonance is a feature of the mantle of the expert approach and enables those elements that are more than facts to be
energized. The words of the oath of Gwalchmai must create experience beyond the everyday. There is an important differentiation for
example in the use of the words "said" and "spoke," the latter being
used for the public declarations and the former for greetings and
directions.

Dorothy's responsibility during the group preparation is twofold.
She can give direct help with a "scene" if help appears to be required,
making sure that it is the *camera* that gives focus to the work, for it
is this concentration on what the camera picks up that removes the
usual self-consciousness of student theatre practice and yet keeps
the "self-spectator" aroused. Again, it is the *camera* that allows the
subtext to be blatantly exploited.

She must also help *indirectly* to keep the beekeeping context
alive. For instance, if the group demonstrating Gwalchmai's love for
his horse were to show him offering the horse hay, she might say,
"I suppose giving him hay and watching if he likes it is a bit like
when we stand in the evening watching the hives all safely closed."
The more Dorothy understands about how mantle of the expert
operates, the more she realizes how language is one of the pillars
upon which the whole experience is built. So statements like "I wonder if they realize what they're asking people like us to do—swearing
oaths under big trees" or "They say their cameras are very big; I
hope they won't make a lot of noise and disturb the bees" or "Bet

they'll like our honey cakes at break time" may seem deliberately mischievous, *but it is this very mismatch of language that creates authenticity and responsibility.* One part of the secret is to live in the present moment of work, ranging over the possible landscapes of forest, urban life, cars, horses, warmth of fires, and central heating. This is often the opposite to the mind-set from which teachers and their students feel bound to operate: the next step . . . the end of the lesson . . . finishing in time . . . tonight's homework. Such a clock-victim approach hardly ever permits serendipity, or the moment's elegance seized fittingly and with grace.

There is no effort to be ready to show work here. Instead it is the small triumph of a "managed moment," which the teacher seizes on to see "what the others think" or "whether they can find it reasonable." There are no effusive apologies for stopping others either! It is the way our enterprise has always worked—inviting others, in our trial and error way, to stop what they are doing for the moment to make comments or give advice; no big deal! Talent is not the issue; the making of meaning *is*.

Day 10, Episode 1

EXTERNAL ACTIVITY

The students decide in pairs how best to demonstrate the contrast between the modern American and ancient British beekeeper at work, using the "bits" inserted into the manuscript and passages/illustrations from the modern handbook.

INTERNAL COHERENCE

The final day and the most complex one, but Dorothy thinks it is worth trying; now that the relationship between student and teacher is so healthy, she believes they can cope with the risk of it not working. Her aim is to help the students realize what they have learned. She is going to ask them to do what historians do, look at and try to explain the details of the past through what they know in the present. Historians never "pretend" to be people in the past—nor will the students.

Making a contract (out of role) —This day begins with Dorothy putting it to the students that they are going to try to understand those times when, many people believe (there is no proof), a king called Arthur reigned in Britain. So a contract was made that everyone would try to take up the stance of modern people who understand bees, explaining how a long time ago people managed their bees: the *dynamic* for the tasks is to reconsider all they know in terms of getting the material in a shape for a BBC television program.

First, the students must reestablish their expertise in the modern establishment—remember the last two days have been spent referring to the "bull" incident and Gwalchmai—by making products from honey. Once they have reminded themselves of their own way of working with bees in their own enterprise, they can work out how they are going to demonstrate this to others, for they decide that contrasting modern and ancient ways makes for a good documentary. And finally they must reabsorb all the information they have about Saxon beekeeping.

In the latter respect, Dorothy has carefully accumulated over the two weeks all the information the students have made or used at different times in their work. Everything is on display in the room when they arrive for the last day. This includes:

1. Pages from manuals about bees and lists of products from bees, plus drawings of various tools, hives, etc.
2. Duplicates of these are attached to the "manuscript" (a central feature of the display) "as if" placed by an earlier archivist.
3. References in their Gwalchmai manuscript mention mead, honey, and medication, and contain some drawings and Saxon illustrations.
4. A plan of their establishment naming the work done in different parts of the site.
5. A plan of the Saxon site, including the large tree.
6. The modern image of the large, broken tree with the bull's horn lodged in it, and the bee swarm, child's cap, and lightning images beside it.
7. Letters from the BBC inviting their collaboration, together with the original blackboard notice about the BBC's interest in finding a group of beekeepers to assist in making the program about Arthur.
8. Their own lists of what beekeepers do to get honey and their own work with bees and hives.
9. All office records and memos from the first week.
10. The tape-recording they made about their work to send to the BBC.
11. Their drawings made from their imagination of life in the

time of Arthur (clothing, hives, heating and cooking arrangements, tools, vessels, containers, bottles), some of which are referred to in the manuscript.

12. The tape-recording of the story of Gwalchmai.
13. The task cards left originally by the BBC rep about the old ways of working with bees: thatched hives, a wooden ladder, lighting a fire to keep mead warm, making vessels to contain honey, mead, foods, racks for tools (wooden ladles, scoops), a mesh to protect bee workers.

Thus all the students' early jottings, listings, and drawings now come into their own—and the students "see" their work and knowledge elevated into a display. Such recycling of student work is a feature of mantle of the expert.

Dorothy, in the role of secretary, explains: *"I thought, as you'll be dealing with the final program, I'd better get all our archives together so that we can check out exactly what we want to put in the program. I hope I haven't forgotten anything. Mrs. Heathcote* [referring to the rep] *said I should try to separate the past-time stuff from our own establishment, but I may not have done it very accurately."* She wanders vaguely (vagueness crisply signed!) between the various display areas as she talks, implying *they* will know what has to be done.

Browsing time —The students need the chance to wander among the displays, reacquainting themselves with their previous work. Here and there they find extra labels with comments. For instance, the note *"We* feed our bees in winter" is placed by the office memo regarding delivery of sugar; the question "Did *they* barter?" is stuck on the unpaid account regarding hives. Each comment on the label carries an implication, while remaining accurate.

Once the browsing has started, the students, in pairs commenting to and planning with each other, move freely about the room. In role as the rep, Dorothy (having laid her secretarial notebook aside for the time being) places herself "on location," in the demonstration area. For those who come close enough to hear, she is musing about cameras: *"I suppose they'll want to use close-ups of some of the work we show them,"* spoken just a bit more publicly than real life, but not so that she is addressing the class. Her contribution too must remain informal, if not casual, in this informal setting, for *the educational exercise for the students lies in the task of creating some kind of statement out of a deliberately unstructured context.* After two weeks of daily working at mantle of the expert, a class (even seven-year-olds) might be expected to find out for themselves what is involved in selecting content for a program. To an outsider, it might look like teacher neglect at this point, but there is a Zen saying: "If you know the target, do not impose your will on the arrow; release it to its flight." The students know the target—they must set about selecting which material is suitable, each pair taking responsibility for reshaping it for camera work. Of course, Dorothy will give help where help appears to be needed—for instance, she will make a "public" list on the blackboard of which aspects are being chosen, as a way of encouraging a range of choices. She also knows that for the actual demonstration she will do some kind of commentating, but she invites the students to guide her as to how she should do it. Though the students are given a "free choice" as to *content,* Dorothy realizes they may need pointers about *form.*

The demonstration for the cameras —Dorothy offers four possibilities: (1) two contrasted portraits of "modern" and "Saxon" beekeepers at work; (2) pairs of workers, standing back to back, occupying their own territory, almost like moving sculptures, ready to demonstrate their work; (3) all the people in modern beekeeping action, and then, by a convention, rolling the centuries back to Saxon times, or (4) each pair in turn to be introduced to the camera to demonstrate first, Saxon, and then, modern, activities. They chose number 4, and Dorothy's commentary offers the following kind of dimension: *"These people, fashioning the ladder to take the* swarm that settled upon a branch of the great oak tree, will *never see those who live after in later times following the same craft."* They work as if for two cameras, one member of a pair explaining, for example: *"To make this ladder, we* realize the people must have known how to make rope and we think that this is what they did. [Action follows]"; the other then takes up the same craft, but now explains: "This is how we do it today." [action follows].

Day 10, Episode 2

EXTERNAL ACTIVITY

The students gather at a high table and draw a "feast of the Dark Ages" on a white paper tablecloth. The BBC rep summarises ("for the cameras") what they have achieved.

INTERNAL COHERENCE

Although this final episode looks different from the preceding experience, it is a coherent development from it. Now the BBC rep is inviting them to gather around the table (which has been covered beforehand with a paper tablecloth, with thick pens—in carefully selected colors—(at the ready). The task for the students now is to *draw* on the paper tablecloth in front of which they are seated a Saxon beekeepers' feast. When all are gathered and started on their draw-ings, the rep talks to the cameras, using the serious tone of a pro-fessional summing up the series. This enables Dorothy to honor all the work of the students while inviting them to "play" at inventing a feast. So they are drawing as she gives a commentary: *"Throughout this series we have been assisted by a group of beekeepers from America, who have given of their time and expertise. While they create with their pens, before the cameras and your eyes, examples of their work and that of people long ago—honey cakes, bottles and jugs of mead made from honey, honey cough medicine and ointments in jars, the flowers that give their nectar, their hives and tools—we shall take our cameras close enough to hear them talking about their work and what they find im-portant about it for people like you and me. Now we can see them draw the work of past keepers, skilled artisans living at the time of Gwalchmai, of Teilesan the harpist, of the Companions, and of the magical sword in the service of Arthur, High King of Britain."*

But these modern beekeepers are on loan to the BBC from their own enterprise, and need to be "returned" there by the question only the BBC rep could ask: "And what will you be working at tomorrow now the program is made?" This is a question that can raise Dorothy's confidence or dash it to the ground and release the black dog that haunts all teachers—that, after all, they have no craft! She can only wait to see if the mantle of the expert system, even in a short time, has generated that sense of responsibility and concern for their en-terprise and confidence to speak their own thoughts publicly. She is not disappointed with the response of this particular class.

Drawing a Few Threads Together

■ **Now that we** have analyzed a range of examples in varying degrees of detail, it would perhaps be useful to attempt to draw out a few theoretical guidelines underlining the practice of mantle of the expert. We will do this under four headings: Emerging Patterns; Theatre Elements; Signing for Authenticity; and Conventions for Making Someone Present.

Emerging Patterns

It can probably be seen now that there is a pattern to mantle of the expert work that emerges as a project develops, no matter what kind of establishment the students are managing.

THE ENTERPRISE BASE

The enterprise convention imposes an obvious and perceivable limit to the domains of responsibility the students will undertake. A modern department store or a monastery or a science laboratory is a world within the larger world, with its own social structure and rules both defining the parameters of responsibility and generating tasks. The tacit recognition by the participants of where the boundaries lie allows them to feel safe—and then to test the limits of those boundaries.

The enterprise, with its assumed past history, can only be created through tasks, those establishing the area of expertise and those dealing with the "new" emerging problem: there is always a crisis around the corner.

WORKING TOGETHER

The "we're in this together" feeling inherent in an enterprise situation, plus the fact that the various tasks are carried out in small groups, achieves a sense of culture. Notice that the feeling of sharing the running of the place is more likely to be achieved by separate small-group responsibilities than if the students are all given the same task—like an assembly line or a chorus line! A greater sense of responsibility is felt within the small groups for completing something worthwhile, and there is a great security in the sense of busyness, with the teacher "bustling about a bit."

This factor of work tasks and responsibility to the business is related to Gavin's earlier question to Dorothy about "good little workers" (see Page 18). The strength of Dorothy's denial derives from the kind of drama a mantle of the expert approach eschews. If you were doing a drama in which the students were to be "good little workers," there would have to be a strong sense of "them" as well as "us," in order to meet the traditional notion of drama as conflict between opposing sides—*us* in conflict with *them*. ("Them" are the enemy, those outside the firm who compete with us or those inside the firm, the "bosses," who oppress and exploit us.) The workplace is represented as a field of battle where workers are concerned with status, working conditions, shared duties and rewards. Now there is a "them" in mantle of the expert work, but of a very different kind. The "them" are our clients, our customers, our neighbors, and our concern is with stature, pride in standards, service, inquiry, and dialogue; the crisis around the corner will create tension, not conflict.

This is more than a matter of taste: **for Dorothy this is a *moral* choice.** She wants our children to have the fulfilling experience, however briefly, of creating a fictional society that cooperates, takes responsibilities, sets high standards of achievement, brings out the best in everyone through committed endeavor. The enterprise world within a world offers them a vision of the possible. Most education is found wanting in this respect and much drama, although well intentioned, focuses on hostility, power, inadequacies, abuses, and repressions: "a vision of human failing," the very essence of tragedy.

DRAMA SOURCES

Whatever the expectancies, the source of the material may be the same, for all dramatic material is inevitably derived from cultural sources. It is worth giving a thought to the different *levels* of cultural input to which drama has access. Professor E. T. Hall, the anthropologist (in *The Silent Language,* New York: Doubleday, 1959), has classified social behavior into three levels *(a) formal,* relating to what a society "stands for" as reflected by its institutions, ceremonies, governing bodies, etc.; *(b) informal,* relating to how its members organize themselves; and *(c) technical,* relating to the day-to-day means individuals adopt for survival. There are many dimensions to life in any society (Hall divides them into such categories as interaction, subsistence, temporality, sexuality, and territoriality). Each of these dimensions can be interpreted at each of the three levels, formal, informal, and technical. Likewise drama can draw on any dimension(s) and at any level.

If we take "temporality" as an example from Hall's list and apply it to "running a monastery" in a mantle of the expert approach, at the formal level the abbot and monks might consider their place in the pattern of God's creation; at the informal level they consider how changes over time affect the fabric of the buildings, the training of the novices, the produce from the soil; at the technical level they consider the day-to-day timetable of their work, prayer and sleep routines. If an alternative to a mantle of the expert approach was employed, the formal level might be the monks seeing God as *angry* and their order as punitive; the informal level might be a *battle* with nature and its seasons; and the technical level might be a feeling of being *oppressed* by the rigidity of the twenty-four-hour timetable. The difference in the two approaches is one of expectancy. In regular drama, with the many tragic themes mentioned above (which Gavin is still strongly attached to!), the feeling of oppression or secret anger provides the subtext for everything the characters do and say. In mantle of the expert drama the subtext is the educational program, the curriculum. There will be no "characters" as such, no simulated feelings, nor the kind of "motivation" that determines individual behavior. The affective element grows out of shared responsibility: *we* run the enterprise in every detail; *we* cope with crises arising from the work; *we* develop our ideas about the work; *we* are the law around here in everything except the law of the land. There is no hierarchy, no heads of department, *and no bosses,* least of all the teacher; as we shall see later in this chapter, the teacher empowers in role and negotiates out of role.

DIFFERENTIAL OF TASKS

Tasks should not be automated or repetitive, because those kinds of tasks limit the range and kinds of decisions and problems that have to be resolved. An automated workplace usually involves workers in mastering closed skills where the demands remain always the same and consequently where the only development can be doing it faster or more accurately. Such work *reduces* the workers, whereas the task experiences they need are of the more open kind where things to be done are always changing in subtle ways. For example, if the enterprise is a bakery or soap works, it is more useful for the curriculum and for the students if most of the tasks relate with hands-on work. Thus Dorothy would run a bakery where speciality baking (e.g., celebratory foods) was a mark of the enterprise. Likewise, in Dorothy's soap factory, the workers would need to be into soaps for sensitive skins, medical soaps, baby soaps, etc.

Theatre Elements

There are a number of theatrical elements that underpin the mantle of the expert system.

THE AUDIENCE

Because the mantle of the expert way of working stresses the doing of tasks, there is a tendency to think that there is no element of art involved. But it is obvious that *any* drama activity must involve drama laws, because those laws are the very bedrock of the activity, especially (and this may come as a surprise) because of the audience—not the direct responding audience in a theatre, but the *sense* of audience derived from the continual awareness of preparing something for a client, or indeed for each other, for scrutiny of each other's work is built in as part of the mantle of the expert system. We talk about *performing* a task, performing, in this case, for two kinds of future audience.

Preparing work for teacher as audience is a common expectation of all educational establishments, but in a mantle of the expert approach the teacher is not an evaluator but a "channeler"—to the client or to other workers and always back to the students, for it is their work, not the teacher's. Some examples may serve to clarify how it works in practice:

1. *Channeling to a future client:* An individual or small group might be told: "I think they'll have placed the order by now—I'll check in the office for you, shall I?" A large group or whole class might be called to a meeting to hear that "we've had an enquiry about such-and-such, and I thought before we invite the rep to call we'd better put our heads together about delivery dates." In both these cases the teacher invokes the "presently absent" client, who, of course, will be the eventual scrutineer of the finished

work. The more the sense of audience is invoked, the better quality of work will be produced.

2. *Channeling to colleagues:* "That's turning out very well—have you had a word with Bill [or, Mr. Somers] about it? Put your heads together and see if he agrees with us." For a larger group it may work like this: "I think it's time we tried this [or, this *idea*] out, don't you? Let's get everybody together and test it properly." In these examples the "audience" is going to be participatory—at the invitation of the task performers.

3. *Channeling to the student concerned:* Wanting greater attention to detail, the teacher might muse: "I hadn't realized how many windows there are in just one house. We could check whether they have to all be the same size and shape: someone said something about standard sizes. I'm not sure whether that means . . ."

4. *Channeling through public notices:* Staff notices may be posted regarding other potential scrutineers—visitors, fire, personnel welfare, or health and safety inspectors; a blood donor service.

Thus, as work progresses, the people carry in their minds a range of "audiences." This creates productive tension.

SIGNIFICANCE

Every spatial arrangement of people and objects is manifested through action and representation. For example, a worker may need a lathe for turning wood. It would not help to "sign" the presence of such a lathe by drawing a flat, two-dimensional picture. Such a drawing would become an embarrassment if it became necessary for the student to demonstrate a work process with the lathe. A more useful indicator would be a "safety notice": the words THIS WOOD LATHE MUST HAVE SAFETY GUARD FITTED DURING OPERATION, accompanied by a drawing of the right/wrong position and the patent number.

Some workers will feel they have more authority if a (paper) socket indicator, enabling them to "plug in," is there beside the notice. It is the immediate expression in action of workers doing tasks that makes the authenticity of these paper representations emerge. For example, it will very likely happen that when lathes are "switched on," workers will be heard making their own machine-noise accompaniment to their simulated actions, as when a young child makes car noises when playing at driving an automobile. It helps to create the automobile or the lathe "in the mind." As a Maori boy said during mantle of the expert work in New Zealand, "This drama is all in your mind, so it feels true."

But of course the main source for authentic SIGNing comes from the teacher. With the precision of an actor the teacher adopts appropriate body attitude, gesture, tone of voice, style of delivery, distance, pitch, choice of vocabulary, deliberate uncertainty or confidence, deliberate vagueness or precision. But whereas the actor defines for the audience the message of the play within the circumstances of the plot, the teacher uses SIGNing as an invitation to the students to join in the encounter, effecting and affecting the enterprise. Unlike the actor, the teacher's purpose is to *empower* the students, who are indeed, at first, merely "audience" to the teacher's signing. Some observers, trapped by their traditional perspective of the teacher/student relationship, cannot see the teacher's input as empowering but as dominating. (More detailed attention to "signing for authenticity" will be given later in this chapter.)

A SENSE OF HISTORY

That the enterprise and the expertise that goes with it have existed in the past is of course confined at first to the teacher's mind. As we have seen in previous examples, she must work hard to use her role to establish this sense of the past: "Like we did last time" or "Have we had this kind of request before?"

FOCUS

As selective as any playwright, the teacher and students evolve a sequence of episodes, not based on plot and subtext as for a script, but on context and curriculum. The mantle of the expert episodes must be faithful to both, as clean and lean as any densely made play. The curriculum areas covered over many months of work may satisfy the most traditional of curriculum devotees in the astonishing spread of topics, but what such a conservative educationalist may fail to recognize is that every aspect of this spread has grown *logically* out of the productive tension of running an enterprise of some kind. It is this *productive tension* that parallels the dynamic of a play as it flows seamlessly from episode to episode. Let us take a brief glance at an example of a year's work covered by a British class of nine-year-olds whose mantle of the expert drama was about *running a shoe factory*. When the work was over the teachers involved were able to categorize the areas of learning for the year:

1. *The gift of a new boiler to replace an antiquated one*

   Science: properties of metals—effects of heat/cutting/jointing/shaping measurements of volume—liquids and solids/ways of joining metals to wood, brickwork, etc.
   Costs: of materials/insurance charges/overheads
   Care: safety rules/routine maintenance/inspections
   Public relations: letters of thanks/speeches at functions/press notices/radio interviews
   Information: instructions for fitting and using the history of the firm that built the boiler writing the biography of the donor
   Art: technical drawing of the boiler the portrait of the donor to hang in the office the brochure of the firm that supplied the boiler

2. *Building the history of the shoe firm, Blackley and Broadene*

   Making the family tree from the time of the first tiny shop in 1868 to the present factory
   Making a scale model of the early building
   Illustrations of shoemakers at work from early times to the present day—tools, spaces, work benches
   Large clay models of 'old workers of the early days' plus their tools and benches
   A catalogue of shoe designs by Blackley and Broadene
   Scenes from the history of the firm for a celebration concert
   Painting of their 'best shoemakers'
   Writing the biography of the first owner of the little shop
   A brochure of working clothes through the ages

3. *A batch of special orders because of the recession*

   Eight sets of elephant shoes for a new film of Hannibal crossing the Alps
   One-hundred pairs of elves's shoes for a ballet company, to be made in green silk with soft leather soles
   Ten leather Roman buckets, replicas to be displayed in the Vindalanda museum

A leather dog harness for eight huskies in an Inuit dog
team
Leather tool belts for divers working on North Sea oil rigs
Interviews on the phone with clients, explaining exactly
how the items will be built
Live interviews with clients about their orders
Technical drawing to show clients the care and
maintenance of goods
Costing and account sheets
Bills to clients with letterhead paper
Postage routes worked out to various countries and
locations (North Sea, Northern Canada, Northern Italy,
Vindalanda Roman Fort, and Moscow)

These lists merely indicate the areas of study. They cannot capture
the excitement and concern operating as workers in "Blackley and
Broadene." For example, when Dorothy, as "Mrs. Heathcote, an ac-
countant from our bank," came to do a thorough inquiry into all their
costs with a view to economizing where possible, the worker's resis-
tance to change (e.g., the suggestion of using coarser wrapping paper
rather than the traditional soft tissue paper in beautiful colors) was
both vigorous and tenacious, including the challenge, "Why does
there have to be change?" Such a question, born in the heat of a
cataclysmic event for their firm, deserves a penetrating answer, leading to more questions: "Because it seems people have to be curious,
always saying to themselves, 'What will happen if . . .?' and then they
try new things."

THE DRAMATIC "NOW"

All theatre relies on events appearing to happen *now*. This is the
essence of the dramatic art form. This "present tense" characterizes
much drama in the classroom too and is central to a mantle of the
expert approach. For it is the existential feeling of *we are running
this enterprise* NOW, with all that that implies for spontaneous interaction with new things that crop up, that creates the productive tension out of which the action and learning will grow.

THE CURTAIN NEED NEVER COME DOWN

Unlike in a play, there do not have to be resolutions, giving the audience a sense of easement out of the fiction. Sometimes, of course, a
class, knowing that the project is coming to an end may want to
"round it off" in their own way. Dorothy recalls an occasion when a

class who had been "running a post office" in a village whose inhabitants, together with their homes, workplaces and histories, had been invented by themselves, decided at the end of the year when school was about to close for the summer holiday, to have an avalanche overwhelm the whole site!

Signing for Authenticity

Suppose we want to turn our classroom into a "tiling factory". The enterprise must feel authentic all the time, even though the whole business is a fabrication agreed upon by the participants. In time the responsibility for making it feel real and truthful will be shared by the students, but at first the teacher carries that aspect of the work. Earlier in this chapter we looked at some of the teacher techniques for establishing, for example, a sense of "we-ness," a sense of past history, and a sense of place. These matters to do with signing now need more detailed attention.

The classroom environment can be modified to a small degree. Furniture can be changed about a little to alter the shape of working spaces. Notices can be placed to remind everybody "what goes on here." Such notices must be *authentic* as to format and message, even though they are made of paper or written on the blackboard. Some will contain direct information, such as TO THE CAR PARK, but others need to evoke a characteristic, to suggest rather than to define. An example of this would be the way the name of the enterprise is established: the workers might choose to invent the name "The Reliable Company" when invited to place a notice so that "visitors might find us."

As the enterprise develops, different areas of wall, window, and floor space as well as arrangements of working surfaces tend to take on definition (e.g., "the office," "the canteen". It is not necessary for a large amount of territory to be taken up by these places—remember it is the office and canteen one sees in one's *mind*. The teacher will readily start to establish these special places: "It'll maybe be in the office" reinforces the notice. A temptation for the regular drama teacher will be to designate some students to be in role as "office staff," but this initial casting of roles limits growth. We say *initial,* for it is conceivable that the need to have someone (notice it is often some*one*) in that role arises naturally from the circumstances, circumstances relating to the social health of the group or a particular educational need rather than the fictional enterprise. It is not uncommon for a child who opts out or is conscious of some lack of skill

• •

(such as reading ability) to find himself "in charge" of a particular place—answering the telephone, for example. It is important that such manipulative devices are recognized as demanding the teacher's extra energies and attention—that children must be strongly supported, perhaps by the teacher in a supportive role as the office manager's assistant, for example.

Which brings us to *telephones! Never* a real one; *never* a toy one! But there are numerous alternatives:

1. *Draw it on a piece of card,* with the pushbuttons precisely marked, and tape the card to a table. Teacher models its use—punching the numbers in the air, *not* miming. (Never mention the word! You want to represent *the urge to telephone* NOT make your hands show they are telephoning. It is the *impulse* you are after not the *imitation.*

2. *Write a notice.* PLEASE BE SURE YOU REPLACE THE HANDSET CORRECTLY AFTER TELEPHONING invites *action.* If a tied pencil and small pad is placed beside it, it also authenticizes the purpose and nature of phoned messages. A wall notice, TELEPHONE, may also be needed.

3. *Post a "phone usage record sheet."* The potential here is for detailed attention to minutes and costs. A drawn clock emphasizes time; a map of radiating lines showing city, state, country, and world has a geographical and distance potential.

Notice how each kind of sign above causes different experiences and different potential for learning.

Warning signs breed crisis. For example, a drawing of a *fire extinguisher* is a crude beginning that can be expanded to a more sophisticated use of warning sign. It can give information about water or spray foam; it can give the name of the manufacturer; it can give capacity and ratings marks; it can give instructions for use. This could grow into having a visit from a fire officer—the school principal in role? It would be possible for "tile workers" to invite the "fire officer" to see their demonstration of tiling in preparation for the new work on the Civic Hall. The responsibility for the tilers is to see their work through the eyes of a professional safety expert. The school principal would play her role with due respect for the tilers' expertise. Or it could be that a real fire officer is invited in. Such a visitor (you may recall that Marianne Heathcote, the student writing at the end of Chapter 5, invited a real monk in to meet her class) would need educating into how to empower the students, not subdue them by her professionalism. Of course, neither visitor may be available, in which case the class will once more resort to "using our colleague Mrs. Heathcote to stand in for a fire officer so that we can test whether our explanations stand up to this kind of professional scrutiny." This may be backed up by a letter from the fire department with an accompanying form to fill in or a blank cassette on which they are to record their safety explanations and then send back to the fire department. (The invitation from the fire officer can be couched in unthreatening language: "You may care to let me know in your own language just the kinds of things your factory does, so that I can advise you about safety precautions.")

This representation of an "audience" through the convention of written questions and spoken replies (we shall be categorizing such conventions in the last section of this chapter) is probably the most efficient for curriculum teaching from within the mantle of the expert structure, because the pace is slower and the mixture of reading, interpreting, and orally explaining what they know is much richer. A tension can be written into the letter from the fire department with a delicately worded hint of a threat and underlined by the teacher's response: "The regulations are getting tougher since [an invented fire catastrophe or a recent genuine one]."

You may wonder why it is necessary to give so much careful attention to the range of conventions available for bringing the outside world in to the enterprise, for we know that the success of the mantle of the expert approach depends on an enterprise being a world within a world. There are broadly two reasons for this: carefully judged interaction with the outside (but not too early in the work, or it will have the opposite effect) *confirms* the existence of the enterprise; and having to see their work through the eyes and professionalism of outside people helps the students to *realise their knowledge.*

One of the most intriguing conventions is to have an object represent an absent person ("presently absent"!). The object can be a clue to the image of an absent person or a clue to the life story of an absent person. Staying with the "tiler" context, imagine that a *briefcase,* not belonging to any of the workforce, is discovered in the office. This can create great tension if the teacher mines the possibilities of the event: Who left it? How did they get in? Should we touch it? Should we open it? Now this looks like an interesting mystery. Indeed if we were "play making," it has all the hallmarks of a most exciting play. But in a mantle of the expert approach there are problems of a different kind: Are our tiling designs safe? What if someone has copied them? Is our safe still locked? Have we simply been inefficient—was someone expected? Is the owner of the brief-case in the building somewhere? In the washroom feeling ill? Trapped somewhere?

If the students' interest appears to lie in the idea of an intruder, then you come *out* of the drama in order to *predecide what the final outcome is to be:* as *dangerous* as they like (an assassin hiding); as *sad* as they like (someone hoping for work or returning to where they used to work); as *challenging* as they like (a plausible thief whom the arrival of the workers has disturbed as he was photocopy-ing). It does not matter *what* outcome they choose as long as they take the responsibility for the choice. The tension then lies not in the shallow one of "what surprise will we get when we find out?" but in the sophisticated one of "we are making this happen to ourselves and we know we have to make it work." This way, it is not the result but the journey that makes for the learning.

The briefcase is the means by which a person is conventional-ized. There can never *be* such a person. If the teacher puts objects inside the briefcase, she is preempting the kind of person it is to be. She may have good reason for seeking permission from the class to impose in this way—perhaps the task she wants to set them is that of logically profiling the person behind the objects.

Here is another example to widen your ideas as to possibilities in the use of conventions. Six-year-old children in the United States were responsible for looking after a dairy herd. This was in the curriculum context of science (grass grows in soil; cows eat grass; grass and cows produce milk; milk must stay clean to drink and to be used as an ingredient in cheese, ice cream, yogurt, cream cakes, and so on). The conventions that enabled them to look after their own cows were a nail head drawn on a card fixed to a wall, with a drawn rope hanging down, and the name of each cow written beside these "signs of our cows." With these in place they had ownership of the dairy. When the cows calved, they added a little nail head and a shorter rope. Their cows' histories were written (as well as a six-year-old herder can) on real paper laid on the floor where the cow "slept." The herd existed within their imaginations, and they gave them loving care. Without the conventions the cows would not have been real enough for the children to cope with the problem pre-sented to them in an encounter with a lady from India, carrying a baby, who wanted to buy a calf from them to take back to India so that her baby would have milk.

A British example: this time the enterprise was "running a na-tional forest." In one difficult area of the forest it was necessary to introduce a huge plow horse. The foresters wanted to feed the horse carrots, and needed to invent a convention that would allow this to happen. So "Michael the Mighty" was represented by four enormous black paper horseshoes laid appropriately on the ground. The way they faced indicated where Michael's head was and their distance apart indicated his size, so everyone knew where to pat him. When it was necessary to work in another part of the forest, the shoes of this best-fed horse in the land were simply carried over the arm of the plowman!

To use conventions of this kind, the teacher needs to understand how to make theatre work, for it is the power of theatre that brings meaning to these signs. So far we have used notices or drawings to indicate objects or people. Sometimes a teacher is lucky enough to use another adult, a colleague, parent, or a friend, as a conventional sign or effigy—which may or may not "come to life." For example, Dorothy was working with a group of students in role as modern gardeners who were to restore a neglected Italian garden. The garden had been made by an early-nineteenth-century lady as a monument to her two dead children, who had been drowned when their bassinet had accidentally overturned near a stream. *The portrait of the lady* stood in the great hall of the house, and they needed to ascertain information from her about the original design, which was also placed in the portrait. The class contracted with Dorothy's assistant that when the gardeners approached for information they would ask: *"Lady, may we enter your time?"* and she would turn her head, rise from the sitting position she held in the portrait, regard the questioners, and step out of the space designated as a frame. When it was needed, the lady would wheel the table with the plan on it out of the picture.

As you try out mantle of the expert you will find that you invent your own conventions for things and people that cannot be there, conventions that will grow naturally from whatever fictional context you are working in. Can you *feel* the excitement of *theatre* in all these possibilities? If you can you will be good at devising signs.

Conventions for Making Someone Present

Dorothy has worked out a categorization of conventions that create another person (actually or virtually present), a person from *outside* the enterprise world, an "other" as she sometimes calls it. As you will see, "others" can range from being naturalistically present (yet SIGNing SIGNificantly, of course!) to being *images* of that person, to being *words* implying a person, to being *a voice* expressing a person, to being *objects* or *signs* left behind by that person.

As we have seen, the tightly knit workforce of an enterprise from time to time (again, not too soon!) benefits from the introduction of someone from outside the operation, an "other"—a professional, visitor, client, whose arrival will never be unexpected; rather the reverse: most carefully planned, so that the "signing" of anticipation is nearly as significant as the arrival.

We will take a particular mantle of the expert example[1] where Dorothy was working with a class of young adolescents. The enterprise was "running a large modern department store." Of course, no single project ever includes *all* the possible conventions. Indeed, *appropriate selection* of a convention is what it is about. But for the sake of this classification we will give examples for the whole range. The common factor will be the department store.

The first thing to remember is that participants must always work from within a frame of influence: expressing a point of view, *needing* to interact with the "other." Where, as in the first category, an actual *person* (teacher in role or teacher's assistant in role) is employed, you must guard against its becoming an entertainment or a peep show or in any way power reducing for the enterprise colleagues, the students.

A Person Physically Present

Meeting face to face (with an architect—teacher in role, assistant in role, or a real architect):

> *Fictional Purpose (frame)*: sent about enlarging the store, which was built in the 1940s.
> *Learning Purpose*: how to read architectural drawings; knowledge of how buildings of the period were constructed.

Directing a film (with the floor supervisor and an interviewer—played by the teacher and a student respectively and directed by the class):

> *Fictional Purpose*: the floor supervisor is giving an account of trying to escape during a fire from a storeroom with barred windows.
> *Learning Purpose*: thinking around a problem of safety.

Effigy (assistant as a "store dummy," perhaps dressed as Santa Clause) (note: it can be walked around and changed around):

1. Dorothy believes the video of this particular work is held in the Department of Theatre, Moscow, Idaho, in the care of Dr. Fred Chapman.

Fictional Purpose: attracting more customers.
Learning purpose: how you can appeal to people by making them notice.

Effigy come to life (assistant as statue in the center of a fountain) (note: it can be talked to!):

Fictional Purpose: a key has been lost in the fountain; we wish the statue could tell us where it is and how it got there (the possibility here of magical or surrealistic encounter—mantle of the expert is so accommodating!).
Learning Purpose: experimenting with a dream sequence or how a statue, with its timeless view of the amazing world of shopping (who knows where its life first started?) gives a new perspective on the shopping mall.

Portrait that can be interviewed (assistant as boardroom painting of the founder of the store) (note: this time he is not three-dimensional to be walked round, but he can step out of the picture frame, and his advice can be sought; also, the whole context of the picture, the subject's surroundings, can be as informative as the portrait; imagine a portrait of Robin Hood with a golden arrow in one hand and a model of a tree in the other, with the names of his followers hanging on "leaves": Maid Marian, Friar Tuck, Will Scarlet, etc., or of General Eisenhower with a row of medals on one table and the oath of allegiance on another, as he is sworn in as President):

Fictional Purpose: some basic change to what the firm has always done.
Learning Purpose: thinking about what the first store owner might have done, faced with these new problems—the meaning of change.

Portrait that overhears (teacher or assistant in role as shop supervisor, with her views of standards of staff appearance pinned into the picture: HAIR SHOULD BE NEATLY CUT OR BOUND SO AS TO CAUSE NO HYGIENE PROBLEM; SHOES SHOULD HAVE LOW HEELS):

Fictional Purpose: shop workers are none too pleased at newly imposed restrictions.
Learning Purpose: as the supervisor concerned is "listening," the complaining discussion among the workers must sound as

reasonable as the new rules. The students thus have to examine the reasonableness of their own arguments, well-enough phrased to keep the portrait listening!

As you become practiced in discerning what the learning areas might be in respect of the various conventions, there will be less and less need for someone else to spell them out for you. Indeed the above "Learning Purposes" are just suggestions from many possible choices. We continue with our classification below, this time leaving *you* to penetrate what learning there might be behind the convention and the suggested frame.

ICONIC REPRESENTATIONS

A slide, a drawing, a painting, a photograph, or a cardboard cutout; may be made by the class or by the teacher.

These can take the form of something as concrete as a photograph—of the original store owner to be used as part of a half-centenary exhibition—or the more fluid opportunity of a spontaneous trial-and-error sketching—of a model employee for an advertising brochure, say; or they can be cardboard cutouts—demonstrating to the present-day workers the garments (*real* clothes) worn by staff when the shop first opened or dressed by the workers using paper clothes made to fit and correct in style.

This latter representation could also be in order, say, for the children's book department to show the story line of the "book of the month" using several cardboard cutouts dressed meticulously according to the description in the book and then called attention to over the "public address system."

SYMBOLIC REPRESENTATION

Clues: clothing or a person's belongings left in disarray—a missing colleague or squatters using the boiler room of the store; deliberately placed clues—someone tampering with goods out of menace or frivolity; a "retrieving" situation, in which a full picture has to be built from a remnant—a tornoff signature or a burnt document.

Associations: in order to create a museum corner of the first owner's life and status, some of his belongings are on exhibition. (You do not have to use expensive objects; they can be simulated—for example, tobacco pouch, diary, cravat.)

PEOPLE BEHIND WORDS

Spoken of: workers are called in to hear of the death of a colleague—someone they all were bound to have met, the doorman, for example;

individuals tell of the virtues of a famous person—a great chef or fashion designer who might be persuaded to attend the official opening of a particular department. The person could be an "invented" one.

Written of: workers are invited to read and comment on an obituary or a reminiscence that the store manager intends to send to the local press about the death of a valued colleague—they prepare the final version; they are invited to respond to anonymous letters impugning staff honesty (not a *particular* member of staff, of course); more formally, they create "the store accident book," covering the past fifty years and including a detailed *report* on an incident affecting a member of the public or staff.

Read aloud about: workers hear the safety officer read his report on new safety regulations for the Maintenance Department personnel; each member of staff reads (with vested interest!) their own departmental report; finding some old record books, one colleague reads out (without any particular vested interest) some of its contents; an application from a job seeker (fictional, of course) is read out.

Overheard: recordings of interactions between customer and shop assistant for the purpose of staff training; the workers make recordings of their own private conversations as guides to new workers to avoid indiscreet or damaging talk that could be overheard by someone else; the workers make their own sound tapes of imagined customer/salesman conversations; a collage of "sounds at night in an empty store" (could lead to dance).

It might be useful to conclude this chapter by reminding you of the twofold purpose of conventions: the explicit use is to bring in an "other" from outside the enterprise; there is a tacit purpose too of protecting students from feeling they are being stared at. Unlike actors, students have not given others "permission to stare." The conventions, however, allow for the point of attention to be away from the participants themselves; they and the teacher together legitimately focus on the physical presence of a visitor or on a drawing or on a costume or property or on a written or spoken message. Only in the later examples in the convention list do they become more exposed through their own creations. As you become more familiar with the conventions, you will realize that one kind can lead logically into another—having read an absent person's letter, for example, the next step might be creating a portrait of her and eventually "meeting" her.

A Final Exchange of Letters

■ **Dear Dorothy,**

This book sprang out of correspondence between you and me about the validity of my bullying lesson as an example of your mantle of the expert approach. It seems appropriate therefore to write you a letter now that the writing has been completed and to include it at the end of this book as a way of both summarizing and questioning further.

When we began I made the mistake, which I am sure others make, of assuming that entry into this approach to drama depends merely on students' adopting an expert role. I saw such a role as a safe way of distancing the student from painful or personal subject matter. For instance, I recall an experienced drama teacher working with older adolescents on the theme they had chosen of "child murder" (there had recently been a local tragedy of this kind). I remember applauding this teacher's common sense in using a mantle of the expert approach by putting the members of the class in role as social workers dealing with the victim's family. I also remember being somewhat shocked and mystified by your obvious misgivings. You did not seem to be impressed by the idea of the students being social workers, and you started to elaborate for the teacher on some much more complex plan that required the students to run a factory that made children's clothes. Thus, the drama about a murdered child was to begin with factory employees designing next summer's fashions; their first task was to try out different colors from a color chart.

By proposing your alternative plan you were not suggesting that it would be impossible for the students to take on social workers; but if they did, I now understand, it would be the *organization* connected with running a social workers' office or a social workers' training school or some other such *establishment* that would become the starting point for the drama, *not,* as in teacher's plan, "social workers interviewing distraught members of the missing child's family."

It has become clear to me that what happens in a mantle of the expert approach is much closer to an actor's becoming a character in a play over several weeks' rehearsal than to the more normal classroom technique of temporarily adopting a role. Whereas it is fairly easy for a student to "switch on" the role of social worker by trying to adopt suitably caring and sensitive actions and language, the *quality* of such role-playing cannot match the gradual absorption, over several weeks' work, of the responsibility and value system that stems from good social worker practice. The difference lies between *describing* and *becoming*. We see this difference in everyday life. Newlyweds might justifiably describe themselves as a married couple, which indeed, technically, they are—and no doubt they set about playing that role. But it will take time for them to *become* a married couple.

I am not of course suggesting that in the mantle of the expert approach students become the experts in any complete way, but I am now realizing that a mantle of the expert approach does take the students much further along the road to engaging with an expert's value system—which is what true learning is about.

Thus, if the participants in the child-murder theme were to be in role as social workers, such role-play should be seen as no more than the equivalent of an actor's first reading—a quick signing of getting into role; the *real* expertise is achieved when the participants no longer need to *signal* expert to each other, because they *are* experts. The analogy with the actor's development of a character only applies to the prolonged period of time they both require, for mantle of the expert is confined to only one type of character, that of a responsible expert, whereas the characters in theatre are limitless.

But, then, so they are in mantle of the expert—at one remove, that is! For once it is established that the students *are* the experts, then *those experts can take on any role of any kind.* If they are to be social workers in the murdered-child drama, they may temporarily assume the role of members of the family or the police or even the victim or murderer but always as a "role within *a role*": that is, it will always be made clear that they are *social workers demonstrating something or trying out something or recalling something.* In the drama teacher's plan, it was expected that some members of the class from time to time would *be* distraught members of the family, etc. It is a curious seeming-contradiction in our makeup that makes it easier to cope with and learn from the temporary holding up of the label "distressed mother" than it is to be confronted with the full-blooded character. One of the things I have learned from writing this book with you, Dorothy, is that authenticity is more likely to be achieved through *in*directness.

This also applies to the knowledge that is to be acquired. It is as if using a directly focused spotlight to illuminate something either merely highlights those features you already knew about or actually takes away the contours and shadows of its meaning—much teaching in school is of this direct blandness. For *seeing it anew,* the spotlight must be beamed through a *prism* and the consequent refraction throws up new meanings.

It is your understanding, Dorothy, of the need for a "prismatic" angling of knowledge that takes you toward the idea of a children's clothing factory as an entry into the murdered-child theme, rather than the more obvious social worker training school idea: establishing that the murdered child was wearing "our factory's clothes," that "we can supply information about color and fabric," and that "our eyes are likely to catch sight of our colors hidden in the undergrowth" will provide a distanced "expert" entry into the distress of the event while exposing information about investigatory procedures.

I have long been familiar with your use of teacher in role, but it is only in writing this book that I have realized it is the *mixture* of teacher/roles, including the normal teacher register, that makes for authenticity. The students can enjoy the ambiguity of teacher playing two or three people, and, again, it is this ambiguity that "disturbs into learning."

Another aspect of the work that I feel at home with is the concept of *empowering* students, so that they gradually take over responsibility for planning their own work. You and I have been conscious as we have written this book that this is a stumbling block for some teachers, because the early stages of the work may appear to be dominated totally by the teacher. The major learning process for the students is that of earning the right to handle more and more complex decisions—again, not because they are labeled experts, but because they are gaining sufficient expertise to make *real* decisions. If the teacher hurries this process, the students' judgments will be derived from their labels, not from their minds.

This brings us to the problem of planning, for in setting up the enterprise (of whatever kind), the students must from the beginning be seen to be making judgments, but not the kind that exposes their inexpertise. It is not just a matter of *making* judgments; there is also the problem of *expressing* judgments, for the students and the teacher may be only too aware of a deficiency in expert language. The means to retain one's balance on this pedagogical tightrope lies in the initial selection of simple *tasks*. The early tasks must be within the range of their *real* judgments and set up in such a way that any inappropriateness of expression (verbal, iconic, diagrammatic, mathematical, or artistic) can be legitimately (if temporarily) overlooked within the fiction. Pitching it right in the beginning for a particular class and for particular students is part of the art of handling this method of teaching, coupled with the need to recognize the pace at which the class can move toward autonomy.

One aspect of the approach that I have yet to think through is your claim, Dorothy, that in using mantle of the expert you are working in *theatre*. I can see connections, parallels, and analogies but certain aspects get in the way of my concluding that, yes, this approach is theatre. Let me first briefly outline the features that support such a view.

Obviously both mantle of the expert and theatre are based on fiction, an initial "lie" so that what follows can be "truthful." As I have argued above, there is a parallel between an actor's building of a character and the building of expertise in the students. One aspect of mantle of the expert that I had not appreciated until sharing this work with you is that everything done in a mantle of the expert approach is *audience* oriented or at least done with a sense of audience—not, of course, an immediate audience to be entertained, as in theatre (although even this is not precluded), but a "client's" or "colleague's" imminent scrutiny. A feature that almost wins me over to believing the work is theatre is the metaphor of "the curtain going up." I find it very exciting that in each of the examples of your teaching described in these chapters, there is an electric moment when the fiction has started and the language used (usually by the teacher) places the participants in the present of *being there* ("there" always being some establishment or enterprise) and, just as important, being there *with a past history*—just like characters in a play, whose language also operates in the present while at the same time creating that past history for the audience.

That the teacher and eventually the students are functioning as playwright is undeniable, not just in respect of language, critical as that is, but in the selection of images that sow seeds of future experience. It seems to me that a defining characteristic of the art form of theatre is that it is caught in the present, bound by the past, and impelled toward the future. A close examination of your method of teaching, Dorothy, constantly reveals that as you discover the present with your students, moving through Act 1, as it were, you are planting seeds for Act 3. But whereas the dramatist's seeds are to do with character development and plot, yours are to do with the development of skills and knowledge or, rather, the extending of the fictional context in such a way that development of skills and learning can occur. Early in your plan for the murdered-child drama you, in role as the manager of the clothing factory, commented on the dangers of the wasteland visible from the factory window; an early task for the employees was to make out a guard roster for the summer holidays "when their children would be out of school." The images of "danger" and "children" were dropped into the colleagues' factory talk, images to be stored for Act 3.

I accept, too, that many of the mantle of the expert experiences are theatrical in their intensity. The participants can have a genuine adventure knowing the outcome but not knowing how the outcome is going to come about. This is not the tension of a whodunit, but rather that of a classical drama, in which the outcome is inevitable: it is the unknown of the journey that creates dramatic tension. But other matters still bug me.

One is that I sympathize with those teachers for whom mantle of the expert cannot be theatre because only intermittently does it look like theatre. Indeed it would distort the approach if the participants themselves saw what they were doing as theatre in any conventional way. This leaves me with a question: if, for the most part, the activity looks like a meaningful learning engagement far removed from theatre, how useful is it to insist that theatre is what it is?

And I have other queries to do with theatre's defining elements. I can accept that the lack of a physically present audience should not provide the grounds for excluding the experience as theatre: I believe theatre is something that can take place between participants without that need to entertain someone else. But I find it hard to include mantle of the expert on the grounds of content and structure. For me, theatre is an art form that seeks the truth by withholding it: one or more characters are constrained to hide their feelings, their hopes, and/or their knowledge of the past. Theatre is, at least in part, about how these constraints are removed. Structurally, the uniqueness of theatre lies in its facility for condensing time. The "now" of a particular event on stage is so highly charged through fine selectivity that any single action is both itself and an instance of itself, resonating with potential meanings. It seems to me that in a mantle of the expert approach most action is and indeed must be in "real" time. The heart of the activity is in the map being meticulously drawn or the notes being sorted or the tabletop being measured. In this the activity is *anti* art.

These arguments all lead me to doubt the desirability of equating mantle of the expert with theatre. And yet there may be an overriding reason for doing so. I am now convinced that mantle of the expert is the most sophisticated and enlightened approach to education to have been devised and that future generations will benefit from its philosophy and practice. And if one asks, What attribute, more than any other, does a teacher need to adopt its principles and methods? the answer lies in a deep understanding of theatre. It is the *conception* that is of the theatre. The way the teacher initiates, builds, empowers, challenges, and perceives what is happening is as a theatre artist and as colleague to the other artists, the students. You Dorothy, use the metaphor of the Lady of Shallott, sitting with her back to the window of her room in the tower, weaving the life that passes by as she sees it through her mirror . . . a more elegant metaphor than my prism.

Mirror or prism or glass held up to nature . . . these are what theatre is and these are the means to education and maturity called mantle of the expert. Thank you for taking me on this journey into teaching through theatre.

Yours,
Gavin Bolton

■ Dear Gavin,

Thank you for confirming what, until we wrote this together, I only intuitively understood. Actually our collaboration on mantle of the expert began years ago because of a chance circumstance that may not have seemed significant to you at the time. I was teaching your experienced elementary teacher's course at Durham University one evening when one of the class members sought advice about "teaching her class about medieval castles." She thought about having the students build a castle in their drama, and I suggested that rather than have them *build* one, they should *repair* one damaged by war. By doing so they would be more able to understand the *purpose* of such strong fortifications, designed to house people, animals, and fighting units and to accommodate water resources and food storage. I also emphasized the *expertise* viewpoint—that she should use the genuine medieval design created by Welshmen renowned for their stocky build and mining and tunneling expertise.

During this discussion, I suddenly realized that ever since Christ-mas—we were now in October—I had been exploring this expertise viewpoint at an intuitive level. At Christmas time my teachers course at the University of Newcastle-upon-Tyne had worked with the members of staff of a small elementary school, at their request, on the theme of the Bethlehem census at the time of the birth of Jesus (perhaps I should explain to readers that in England religious worship and education is a *compulsory* part of the curriculum in state schools). The teachers wanted my students and me to find a way of setting the stable and crib (of which they had made a model) against the background of a population count. The whole school was to be involved.

I found myself working with three so-called naughty boys, and we were to make the journey of the Magi from their distant lands to the inn at Bethlehem. Other groups were creating the Roman census officials; King Herod and his court in Jerusalem; the soldiery; the innkeepers; the Holy Family; the shepherds and the angels who, according to the scriptures, appeared to them in the fields; and, finally, the people of the land of Israel.

The three boys became kings, and I functioned in role as their servant as we journeyed from their observatories, following the star. The journey was created in a series of episodes: sighting the great star; making wills in case we did not return; realizing we had to pay for water in desert lands; bartering for a camel to replace a sick one; meeting Herod; and so on. When we arrived in Bethlehem all was quiet at the inn, as the census was over. The star led us to the Holy Family.

During that week I had realized, but not yet fully understood, that it was the *tasks* we did on our journey as Magi that created the power, curiosity, and vulnerability of the three wise men: *Watching* stars and finding new ones established our interests. *Making* our wills before departure helped us to realize we were leaving valuable and unique equipment to be cared for in our absence. *Grooming* the camels, *guarding* the precious gifts of gold, frankincense, and myrrh, and *bartering* for everyday needs became the means whereby three "naughty boys" grew in dignity and stature as the week progressed. Gradually they began to define *my* work as their servant. I had never had such an interesting philosophical discussion with children as we "settled down each night under the stars."

I began to realize that this "expertise of viewpoint" could help teachers with little conscious understanding of theatre to get things started *under* the story line instead of merely replicating the narra-tive. Also, because children enjoy playing at "busy authority" (as younger children enjoy "playing house"), the work could be launched via short, precise, honed-for-the-purpose tasks relevant to the theme. (For example, in this Bethlehem census work, Roman soldiers burnished their parade armour and underwent a parade inspection before packing for the march to Bethlehem.) Finally, making the teachers look for episodic development of the work over a period of time enabled the children to work as individuals within a whole-group enterprise, which provided controls yet allowed children and teachers to feel the work had purpose. This made for a new enthusiasm and feelings of security: the teachers felt it "went well," the children didn't feel "stared at."

Then I came to work with your group on planning, and placed two ideas side by side:

1. Actors need a vast amount of knowledge in creating their roles and interpreting the life-style and period of the plays they interpret and perform.
2. Students come to school to learn; drama and theatre provide contextual parameters that invite and require research.

Mantle of the expert does not take the place of theatre-oriented work. Nor does it challenge the theatre teaching traditionally found in school. It uses the same laws: people wear their "mantle" (i.e., express their interests, habits, and style) in juxtaposition with others in active expression. They use their expertise and knowledge to move along different highways: the actors project personality and bondings *with* others *to* others who are watching; the students actively bond *as* colleagues set on tasks *to* supply their clients (the "audience in the mind"). It would be as ridiculous to ask actors to do the latter as it is to ask students to achieve the former (before their needs as performers make them ready to learn this craft, that is).

The two highways can occasionally meet—as when, for example, students need to experience the pressure and *excitement* of an event directly (as in the "tiger hunt" in Chapter 8) or when actors may need a direct, swift *understanding,* as opposed to an *explanation,* of, say, the Globe or Swan theatres of Shakespeare's time. Creating a short, self-contained mantle of the expert session where the actors, framed as hoping-to-be-hired extras, may meet Mr. Burbage, and, in being conducted around the theatre, can realize in a unique way how the building and the play have a symbiotic relationship.

Thinking along these lines firmly began on that evening in the

University of Durham with that moment at serendipity when "wise men" and "castles" met in my mind. We've come a long way since then.

Regarding your doubts about equating theatre and mantle of the expert: it is a myth that I have done so. I see the *laws* of theatre expression—the seen and the not seen, the spoken and the withheld, the still and the moving, each dimension expressed SIGN*ificantly*—as applying to both. You are right when you see *time* as being differently used. I can sum it up this way: the human face is usually possessed of a mouth, a nose, two ears, and two eyes, with surrounding bits to join these elements together. The bits that join and surround create the communicating system of the face. Theatre has many "communicating faces" that surround and give a variety of shapings to a few operant laws:

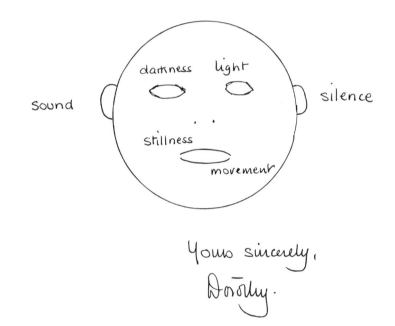

Yours sincerely,

Dorothy.

Appendix A
The Bishop's Letter

Greetings to all the Benedictine monks in your Monastery!

As Bishop of the Holy See of Chichester it is my desire to found a holy house of women in Chichester Cathedral, to be called the Nunnery of St. Mary Magdalena. I would like to give them a very special gift of a book to assist their understanding of the way of life of the Benedictines. Your fame as illuminators and writers of books has spread even to us so far south in Chichester. Therefore I am asking you to do us the great honour of creating one of your most special manuscripts for our good nuns in Chichester. Our nuns would need to know about life in a holy house dedicated to God's service, such as yours is, according to Benedictine rules. They need to know what duties are performed by your monks in the different positions which they hold and what problems they may meet. Please could you also include in your special manuscript details of the rules of your Benedictine order, as well as information about the division of your day and the services you attend.

I have seen manuscripts which have been made by you, finely illuminated with beautifully patterned borders and illustrations. We would be greatly honoured if you produced such an illuminated book as the nuns require. I have heard that you are already extending your scriptorium to give more space and light for your writing and manuscript work, and I am sending with this parchment 100 gold pieces so that the extension work can be completed.

I shall come to your Benedictine
monastery on the <u>27</u>th of January
to receive this most special book.
I am, as always,
   your Brother in Christ

Bishop Anselm.

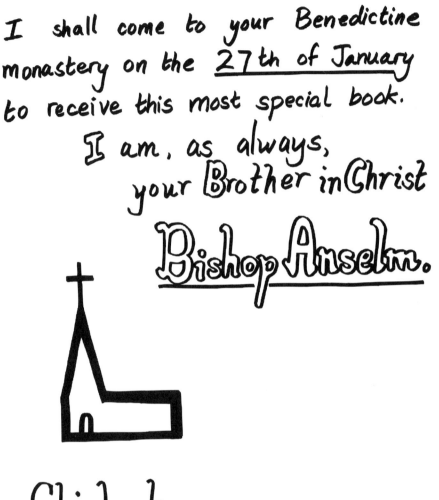

<u>Chichester.</u>

Appendix B
Monastery Floor Plan

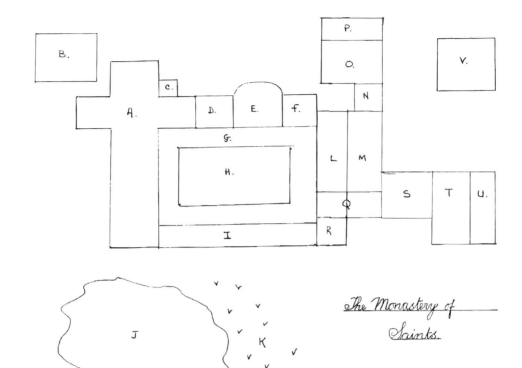

The Monastery of
Saints.

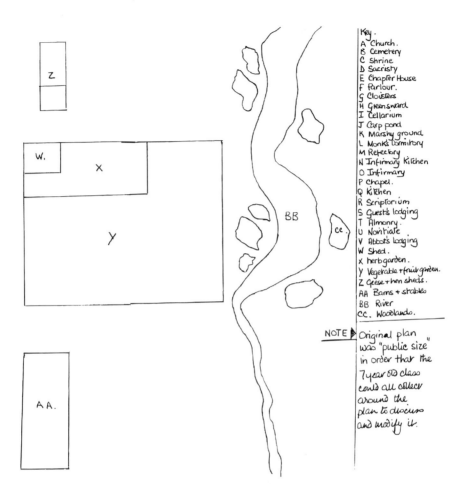

Key.
A Church.
B Cemetery
C Shrine
D Sacristy
E Chapter House
F Parlour.
G Cloisters
H Greensward
I Cellarium
J Carp pond
K Marshy ground
L Monks dormitory
M Refectory
N Infirmary Kitchen
O Infirmary
P Chapel.
Q Kitchen
R Scriptorium
S Guests lodging
T Almonry.
U Novitiate
V Abbot's lodging
W Shed.
X Herb garden.
Y Vegetable + fruit garden.
Z Geese + hen sheds.
AA Barns + stables
BB River
CC. Woodlands.

NOTE ▷ Original plan was "public size" in order that the 7 year old class could all collect around the plan to discuss and modify it.

Appendix C
Some Notes on Chamber Theatre, Plus the Complete Script for "The Rescue of Teilesan"

Robert S. Breen, in his codifying discussion of chamber theatre (*Chamber Theatre,* New York: Prentice Hall, 1987), defines the form this way: "Chamber theatre is dedicated to the proposition that the ideal literary experience is one in which the simultaneity of the drama, representing the illusion of actuality (social and psychological realism), may be profitably combined with the novel's narrative privilege of examining human motivation at the moment of action" (p. 5).

Not having a suitable text from which to generate the narrative she needed for the eighth session of the "King Arthur of England" work, in which she wanted her students to live through a portion of the story "as it might have been," Dorothy had to create one. If she had been working within the context of regular school classes, she and the children would have used language periods to create the account of "The Rescue of Teilesan," and then, in discussion, work out who would have reason to tell the story. Thus they would have together first elaborated a novella and, after agreeing on the completed version, then decided on the narrator's identity and point of view.

However, in this case Dorothy had to select the narrator beforehand. She chose a Companion's wife—the word spreads through oral tradition! Then too, chamber theatre rehearsal time is normally spent *with the text firmly in the students' hands* and the text informs and guides the action. This priority also had to be dispensed with. In the single morning session the time was spent immediately trying out action to fit the narration.

The Rescue of Teilesan

The narrator, Eivlin, wife of Rhys ap Sion, one of the Companions, is seated with a scroll. Teilesan I sits apart with his harp upon his knees. Gwalchmai I sleeps throughout the storytelling, Teilesan II standing beside him. Gwalchmai II is with the Companions. Each person wears his name upon his tabard. The tunic/tabards are made of white paper pinned on their shoulders and tucked into their belts or trousers. The actors who will represent those people in the dream who are not Companions—oarsmen, merchants, travelers, beggars—are gathered in another part of the stage.

NARRATOR *(stands and moves to the sleeping Gwalchmai):* Greetings! I am Eivlin, wife of Rhys ap Sion, one of the Companions of Arthur, erstwhile High King of Britain, now lost in battle some do say. Others say that he was taken to the Islands of the Blessed to rest until such time as the great sword and stallion shall be needed on our earth. Gwalchmai, who lies here sleeping, once dreamed a dream of how he and the Companions rescued the great bard Teilesan. *(She moves to Teilesan I, who cannot see her)* See then this dream of Gwalchmai as the Companions remember it, now that there are no more battles to be fought beside their High King. Gwalchmai in his dream *(Gwalchmai I rises as in sleep)* saw the Companions . . .
GWALCHMAI I: . . . standing in a boat. *(The Companions move into a boat shape)*
NARRATOR: The oarsmen were rowing briskly. *(Two oarsmen step forward and begin to row. Teilesan I gently strums his harp)*
GWALCHMAI I: The companions sought Teilesan, harpist to Arthur. *(He lies down again and sleeps until the end)*
NARRATOR: He had been captured in battle and taken . . .
COMPANIONS: . . . to Less Britain. *(The oarsmen stop, leap out, and hold the boat while the Companions step out with Gwalchmai II)*
GWALCHMAI II: Let us leave our weapons and all signs that we are warriors. *(They leave their [imaginary] spears, shields, and [paper] tabards in the boat and the oarsmen take it away, rejoining their group)*
NARRATOR: Then began a weary search. *(The Companions move as a group as if wearily walking)* They came into a town. *(The group of merchants and travelers rise and call their wares, hurrying about buying and selling. The Companions move amongst them)* . . .

VARIOUS COMPANIONS: . . . asking of Teilesan.

NARRATOR: Some described and some showed . . .

COMPANION: . . . his way of walking *(Walks as if Teilesan)* . . .

COMPANION: . . . noble yet not arrogant. *(Walks as if Teilesan. Teilesan I watches and smiles and strums a loud chord, as a commentary)*

NARRATOR: Others of the Companions told of his great red woolen cloak, showing . . .

COMPANION: . . . how it flowed about him *(Moves and shows)*.

COMPANION: . . . how he used it as a blanket against the cold *(Moves and shows)*.

COMPANION: . . . how he hid his harp from thieves *(shows)* . . .

COMPANION: . . . and weather *(shows)*.

NARRATOR: Many times they asked *(The merchants melt back into their group again)* . . .

COMPANIONS: . . . and were disappointed. *(They walk on and sit down dejectedly. Teilesan I plays soft, tired chords)*

NARRATOR: Gwalchmai of the Light bade them. *(Gwalchmai II rises among the companions)* . . .

GWALCHMAI II: . . . rise, bind up your weary feet *(They do so)*, and let us . . .

COMPANIONS: . . . continue on our way.

NARRATOR: All people they met upon the way knew nothing of the bard Teilesan *(Travelers rise and meet the companions, then return to sit with their backs to the audience again)*. There came a day, when, standing beside a fortress they heard *(A traveler rises)* . . .

COMPANION: . . . a passerby *(The traveler walks as if carrying a tray upon his head)* . . .

COMPANION: . . . a lad with loaves and mead . . .

COMPANION: . . . whistling. *(The "boy" whistles a tune and all turn to watch him. Teilesan I plays the tune softly)*

NARRATOR: The tune upon his breath was . . .

GWALCHMAI II: Teilesan's song! *(He catches the boy)*

COMPANIONS: The very one. *(They all move toward the boy)*

NARRATOR: Gwalchmai and his friends gathered around the lad and asked him where he . . .

GWALCHMAI II: . . . learned that song.

NARRATOR: The boy stopped and Gwalchmai gently said . . .

GWALCHMAI II: Set down the tray.

NARRATOR: This he did *(The boy does)*, though he was afraid and cowered as if caught in some wrong act. A Companion spoke gently to him and took his arm . . .

COMPANION *(doing so):* . . . we mean no harm . . .

COMPANION *(touching the boy gently):* . . . that song . . .

NARRATOR: At this the boy stood up and looked about him, drawing the Companions into a narrow street away from the people who began to gather *(Teilesan I accompanies with strong chords on the harp as crowd of onlookers move toward them)* . . .

ONLOOKERS: Is there some trouble here?

Why do you accost the boy?

He does no wrong.

The barley bread and mead . . .

. . . are his to take . . .

. . . for they are paid for at the inn.

NARRATOR: And Gwalchmai stepped forward and spoke to all the people *(The harp gently slows to quietness)* . . .

GWALCHMAI II: Friends . . .

NARRATOR: . . . he said, and spoke them fair . . .

GWALCHMAI II: . . . we heard the tune and recognize it as from our country of Great Britain.

NARRATOR: A Companion, my husband Rhys ap Sion, noted for his gentle looks, then said . . .

RHYS: We travel far from home and to hear that song here in your country took us by surprise.

NARRATOR: At this, the people gathered close to hear what else Rhys had to say. *(They move about Rhys)* Instead of words he whistled gently the same tune as the boy. The crowd murmured among themselves . . .

CROWD: The same tune as the boy . . .

NARRATOR: . . . and they were more curious still to know . . .

CROWD: What's special about that tune?

TEILESAN II *(Shaking his head):* What's special about *my* song? *(They don't, of course, hear this)*

NARRATOR: Gwalchmai saw that he must give a further explanation, but was perplexed about how best to speak, yet tell no secrets regarding who he and the Companions were and whom they sought. Finally, he said, pointing to Sion . . .

GWALCHMAI II: My friend here seeks for his father, an old man who traveled here with mead and flour to sell.

NARRATOR: And as she spoke, all the Companions nodded in agreement but kept close to the boy *(They do so)* while Rhys picked up the boy's jug of mead and tray *(He does so)* and held it out, saying . . .

RHYS: The very things my father sells, and now this boy has heard his tune, for how else could he know it?

NARRATOR: The crowd were thoughtful and began to talk amongst themselves, while Rhys restored the bread and jug of mead into the boy's hands *(He does so; Teilesan plays his tune very softly)* and Bedwyr of the smiling face stepped forward *(He does so)* and bowed with courtesy, saying . . .

BEDWYR: If you would step aside a little so we may speak of this matter to the boy, we may discover something to enable us to find this dear old man who is so precious to our friend here.

NARRATOR: At this the crowd moved away, looking over their shoulders as if to reassure themselves that Bedwyr spoke the truth. The Companions drew the boy down and sat beside him, careful not to crowd him nor spill the mead or tilt the barley bread from off the platter. *(The crowd and the Companions do these things as the Narrator describes them)*

NARRATOR: And Rhys ap Sion spoke softly to the boy . . .

RHYS: Have you seen a tall old man, with a great red cloak hereabouts?

NARRATOR: The boy's eyes lit up and glancing at the crowd *(He does so)*, he drew close to Rhys and Bedwyr, whispering *(He bends closer to them)* . . .

BOY: Are you the Companions who seek the bard Teilesan?

NARRATOR: Their excitement was great, but they gave no sign, except to glance about them at the great wall which towered above them, then at the crowd who yet waited. Afterwards, when Rhys was safely home and sitting at our hearth fire, his own horn of mead in his hand *(Rhys moves close to the narrator and everyone else freezes)*, he said . . .

RHYS: Wife, I tell no lie, it was a time to make us sweat for we could give no sign that we had understood the boy . . .

NARRATOR: . . . and added . . .

RHYS: . . . furthermore, we longed to dance and shout, but that the crowd were yet suspicious that we meant to harm the boy.

NARRATOR: This he told me of, but at that time his telling me lay in the future, and they were yet in danger. So Cei stepped forward, saying to the crowd . . .

CEI: Is there some inn hereabouts where we can share a jug of mead or ale, or any of that wine we have heard tell you make in Less Britain?

NARRATOR: At this the crowd were pleased and led the Companions to an inn close by *(They crowd in and silently drink together. Some become servants and serve the others. The Companions pay)*, pleased to learn more of the travelers and the old man they sought. But one man stood suspiciously aside, watching carefully how Bedwyr and Gwalchmai led the boy to a buttress in the wall. *(They do so, and a man draws close to them)* Rhys, my husband, watched that man, and so carried the boy's bread and mead to where he could stand between the Companions and the man he considered to be perhaps a spy. *(He does so)* Gwalchmai and Bedwyr then asked the boy if he knew . . .

BEDWYR: . . .where Teilesan the bard is now?

NARRATOR: For answer the boy glanced meaningfully toward the great fortress high above their heads. He turned away and drew upon the ground with his finger in the dust a barred window, saying into Bedwyr's ear . . .

BOY: They have him deep in the dungeons where no one may visit him but I who am allowed to bring him food.

NARRATOR: And Bedwyr spoke, quietly, yet his mind was filled with horror at Teilesan buried in stone, and said . . .

BEDWYR: And he is well?

NARRATOR: The boy described how the walls did run with water so that damp ferns grew in the cracks, and told of . . .

BOY: . . . rats that ceaselessly ran about the floor and the cries of others, prisoners like himself.

NARRATOR: The two were horrified by the tale the boy told, and asked . . .

BEDWYR: Can you lead us to this place?

NARRATOR: The lad shook his head and said . . .

BOY: Only I can pass the gate except on days when beggars come to kill the rats for food.

NARRATOR: At this my Rhys pricked up his ears and looked to see if the watcher also heard. *(He does so)* He began to hum a tune *(He does so)* to cover any words the boy might say. And Gwalchmai bent closer to the boy and asked him . . .

GWALCHMAI II: Can you show us the way into this place, but bring no harm upon yourself?

NARRATOR: The boy said he could make a map to show the way, but cautioned them about . . .

BOY: . . . the guards who keep the keys, whose orders are that only food and drink could enter, and on certain days, dead rats might leave in beggars' bags.

NARRATOR: Bedwyr and Gwalchmai whispered in his ear two things. Bedwyr asked if he would say to Teilesan . . .

BEDWYR: Bewyr sends you greeting.

NARRATOR: . . . and Gwalchmai that . . .

GWALCHMAI II: Teilesan is not forgotten. Bid him listen for the song.

NARRATOR: They then arranged to meet the boy later at the inn, when he had taken his load of mead and bread to Teilesan and the other prisoners. And Rhys gave him back his tray and called the Companions from within the inn. *(The boy leaves and sits among the* *crowd with his back to the audience)* The listening man had left the shelter of the wall, leaving them . . .

RHYS: . . . uncertain if he was friend or foe.

NARRATOR: The Companions left the inn and all together they gathered to consider what to do. Gwalchmai spoke quietly, while Rhys ap Sion watched, and said . . .

GWALCHMAI II: Friends, beggars' clothes it has to be: but we must exchange these travelers' cloaks for rags and scraps, and go barefoot into the hideous place, and whilst killing rats, kidnap Teilesan thence.

NARRATOR: They all agreed, but none were happy to do the slaughtering. They made their plans: first to find beggars who would take their woolen cloaks and give them in return their filthy rags. So they walked about the town as if they were admiring strangers, and at last came upon a group of beggars crouched about a meager fire. *(The crowd become beggars; the Companions walk about appropriately)* And Gwalchmai, with Bedwyr at his heel, approached and said . . .

GWALCHMAI II: We are merchants intent on a sport. Will you exchange your rags for these cloaks and other clothes?

NARRATOR: The beggars were suspicious and came *(They do so)* and looked them up and down, fingering the fine wool of their cloaks and doublets. Then they whispered among themselves, until a bold one spoke . . .

BEGGAR: Rich men do not often seek us out. Can you swear you mean no harm?

NARRATOR: And all the Companions placed their hands on their hearts and swore, saying . . .

COMPANIONS: This we swear.

NARRATOR: And drawing further from the fire they exchanged their cloaks for beggars' rags. *(They do so)* The boy came back and waited for them at the inn and was amazed at what he saw until Gwalchmai sang the tune of Teilesan. *(He does so, while Teilesan II plays the tune as well)* Then the lad drew in the sand outside the inn the plan that they should follow and warned them that . . .

BOY: The guards will count you in and count you out and watch you while you kill and bag the rats. I gave the bard your message as I promised, and he heard.

NARRATOR: And he asked them had they knives. And they showed him how in their doublets *(They half draw their weapons)* their battle throwing-knives were kept. And he led them to the entrance to the fortress, which was at the top of many stairs. *(They "climb," following the boy)* He beat upon the door *(He does so)* and hid himself *(he does so)* to wait and guide them swiftly down. The door opened from within *(it does so)* and a surly guard stood there. *(One of the crowd* *takes a position as guard)* Rhys, my man, stood forward, for of all the friends he was most good at pranks of voice-disguising, and spoke in his best beggar's voice, the one as if he had no teeth to bite his meat with. Often he had King Arthur's hall agale with laughter with this prank at Lammastide or harvest when the mead horns went around the board.

RHYS: It is the time when we must come to take our share of rats, with winter coming on and that . . .

NARRATOR: And to their joy, the door was opened wider and some other guards came forward *(They do so from the crowd)* and watched each one as they entered the dark labyrinth. *(They walk past guards and feel their way around many turning tunnels, making rat sounds. Teilesan II moves to sit alone, after taking the harp from Teilesan I and placing it behind him)*

NARRATOR: As they walked and felt their way deeper and deeper into the labyrinth, Gwalchmai softly sang Teilesan's song. *(He does so and they circle close to Teilesan who answers with a soft chord upon the harp)* The chord guided them and they are IN! Stopping only to whisper their names, they set about killing rats. *(Each man touches Teilesan, who stands with his harp, and amidst squeals and grunts they strike the rats)* And when the pile grew large, instead of placing them into their great bags, they put the harp (beloved of Teilesan, given to him, so rumor said, in the Islands of the Blessed by Lugh of the Light) into one bag. Then, the smallest of them all, my Rhys of course, gave his rags up to Teilesan and climbed into the other bag. *(all these actions they do)* Taking some rats into their hands to scare the guards, who feared the plague brown rats can bring, they made their way, one with Rhys slung over his shoulder, to the great door, where the guards watched them closely and counted each "beggar." *(This they do)* Then the great door closed behind them and the boy came from his hiding place and led them down. When they were free of the great fortress, my poor Rhys was released *(It is done)* to breathe fresh air and they, barefoot as they were, set out to find the seashore and their ship. *(The boy stays with them; Teilesan II takes his harp and they sing the song of Teilesan as they walk to the shore; rowers come with the boat and they climb aboard still singing)* These are the words they sang:

> "The sea breaks upon its strand
> And throughout earth's ages still it sings
> Each wave its music rings upon the sand
> Undecaying, deathless . . . free."

(They hum as the narrator speaks. She rises and goes to Gwalchmai I. He opens his eyes and slowly rises. Teilesan I takes the harp from Teilesan II, who is in the boat. All in the boat freeze and Teilesan I stands by Gwalchmai I. Teilesan I, Gwalchmai I and Eivlin say together) This was the dream of Gwalchmai.

The Value and Methodology of Chamber Theatre

The appeal to Dorothy of chamber theatre lies in the fact that *showing* a story becomes possible. The narrator tells and holds the form, while the showing involves the actors in the demonstration of action. Because the narrator tells the motivation and impulses of the people in the story, the actors are freed from the burden of carrying those feelings. All they are required to do is give a crude "sign" of what the feelings might be; for instance, in the Gwalchmai script, a stage direction indicates that "they sit down dejectedly."

An interesting feature, especially relevant to an educational context, is that while leaving the responsibility of *expressing* the underlying motives and feelings to the narrator, in order to function the actor must nevertheless *understand* those motives and feelings. Thus, paradoxically, the students may feel strongly the tension of the event, picking up by osmosis the feelings of the characters as described by the narrator *because* the burden of having to express those emotions is removed. The narrator almost invokes the feeling and emotion in the students as they demonstrate the behavior that conveys the story.

Chamber theatre can be developed by teacher and students in close collaboration as they work out their ideas. The Gwalchmai story was deliberately designed to use all the group, girls and boys, calling Gwalchmai's fellow Knights "Companions" thus avoiding a gender problem, and used two Teilesans and two Gwalchmais to show how chamber theatre permits conventions to be introduced that are not possible in naturalistic theatre.

Sessions such as this enable the teacher actually to instruct about how theatre works, in particular the notion of "self-spectator." Thus, in one leap, the form of mantle of the expert allows a shift from enterprise colleagues to theatre-making colleagues.

As we have already said, this was not a typical example of chamber theatre work for various reasons. Dorothy, in making the taped story of Gwalchmai, had introduced the possibility of an adventure (the rescue of Teilesan from a dungeon) in case the students were interested in that kind of drama work. They did in fact choose the rescue episode from their own script, which read baldly, something like: "The Companions rescued Teilesan in a dream and there were rats." Because of the shortage of time Dorothy both selected which "voice" (that of Eivlin, wife of Rhys ap Sion, one of the Companions) should be *narrator* and created the script herself.

In more favorable conditions, the primary value of chamber theatre work lies in the way participants must scrutinize the written text in order to clarify what parts represent action and talk and attitude. Because the action part of the narrative will be demonstrated by people moving in space and immediate time, it is essential that they decide by careful reading of the text who is the *narrator* and what is that person's *investment* in telling the account. This forms the guiding principle of the dramatic action and causes the participants to penetrate the author's intention and point of view much more deeply than a review of the story line.

An example of the "narrator" decision can be seen in a very simple, anonymous nursery rhyme:

> Jack and Jill
> Went up the hill
> To fetch a pail of water
> Jack fell down
> And broke his crown
> And Jill came tumbling after

Who is telling the story and why? would be the basis of the first discussion. This immediately elevates a factual account into a human dilemma. Twelve-year-old students, in considering this rhyme, worked out a chamber theatre version in which a group of neighbors carried two dead children and their buckets to their parents. The narrator was seen as a grandmother showing a future generation of children a marble churchyard monument of two children with buckets (*real* children as statues). The chamber theatre version went thus:

Jack and Jill [*narrator points to monument*]

[*two ghost figures dressed exactly like the children in the monument move into view with their buckets*]

Went up the hill [*Jack and Jill walking*]

[*Their mother calls*] To fetch a pail of water [*The children work the well pump at the top of the hill*]

[*Jack falls in and Jill tries to help*]

[*Neighbors come running and get the children out*]

· ·

[*They are dead; and are carried by the neighbors to their parents' cottage*]

[*Narrator, as they pass by in ghostly procession, says to her real grandchildren*] Jack fell down

[*Neighbors say to mother at cottage door*] And broke his crown

[*Mother asks*] And Jill?

[*Neighbors answer*] Came tumbling after

[*The grandmother and children gaze at the monument and the procession of ghost neighbors and family go by the church carrying two coffins. The children and the grandmother chant the nursery rhyme softly as they look up at the monument.*]

You might like briefly to examine the following written accounts as if you were about to turn the events into chamber theatre, asking yourself the two basic questions:

1. Who is the narrator?
2. What is that person's investment in telling the events?

The first is from an account of the sinking of the Titanic (Robert D. Ballard, *Exploring the Titanic,* London: Pyramid Books, 1988), the second from *Fabled Lands* (New York: Life Time Books, 1986).

> On Wednesday, April 10, 1912, the *Titanic*'s passengers began to arrive in Southampton for the trip to New York. Ruth Becker was dazzled as she boarded the ship with her mother, her younger sister, and two-year-old brother, Richard. Ruth's father was a missionary in India. The rest of the family was sailing to New York to find medical help for young Richard, who had developed a serious illness in India. They had booked second-class tickets on the Titanic.
>
> Twelve year-old Ruth was delighted with the ship. As she pushed her little brother about the decks in a stroller, she was impressed with what she saw. "Everything was new. New!" she recalled. "Our cabin was just like a hotel room, it was so big. The dining room was beautiful—the linens, all the bright, polished silver you can imagine." (pp. 12–14)
>
> **A Parting of the Worlds**
> The tale began with a shepherd who was whiling away a summer's afternoon on a hillside near the parish of St. Mary's

about five miles from Bury St. Edmunds. He sat in the shade of an oak copse, surrounded by his sheep. In the valley below the hill, the men and boys of the village were busy at the haying, and the shepherd could hear faint shouts or laughter from time to time. But the air among the trees was mostly quiet, except for the buzzing of flies around the sheep and the chirping of crickets.

Then the sheep flicked their ears inquiringly as a soft cry broke the peace. It was followed by a high-pitched, frantic whispering. After a few moments, when the whispering did not cease, the shepherd rose to his feet with a grunt. He ambled off through the trees in the direction of the sound.

The whispering came from an abandoned wolf-pit higher up the hill—a bowl of hard, red earth, rimmed with brambles, where wolves that threatened the town once were thrown and left to die. The place was thought to be haunted. Reaching the edge of the pit, the shepherd stared down in astonishment.

Huddled at the bottom were a boy and a girl. Except for their fragile slenderness, they had the shapes of any children in the shepherd's hamlet. But they were clothed in leaves and flowers, and their flesh, more translucent than a human child's, was the delicate green of the young willows that bent by the banks of the Ouse in spring. Moreover, the tendrils of hair that curled around their faces were as green as the river reeds.

What kind of ideas have come to your mind as you read these texts? Who have you picked as a narrator for the Titanic text? Obviously the author has a lot of diverse information, not only about the ship (the decks, the size of rooms, the silver) but also about the people, their reason for sailing, and Ruth's personal response to the occasion (dazzled, impressed, delighted). This may have suggested Ruth herself as narrator—perhaps in old age remembering the start of the voyage in Southampton. You might then have considered the second question, her *investment* in recounting her memory.

You will have noticed perhaps that the narrator speaks *of* Ruth in the first section, so that may have caused you to think again about Ruth as narrator. Perhaps a life-size painting of the quayside, the *Titanic,* and the hordes of people could be the context? In a museum? A curator explaining details to tourists? People can then step out of a painting to demonstrate the events as they are recounted. And did you consider how the ship could be conveyed—perhaps by the way the crowds and Ruth's family board it and disperse themselves? How to demonstrate the different concerns of the family members: the younger brother's serious illness, perhaps the mother's anxieties in settling everyone into the days of voyage, Ruth's delight and independence in exploring, yet being responsible for her baby brother?

How will you deal with the "recall" statements of Ruth if the curator is your narrator? These are the sort of problems that can suddenly confront you as you carefully 'interrogate' the text to find crucial centers of narrator and investment. You might have changed your "painting" for a "photograph"—of Ruth's family with luggage, waiting to board. Who *needs* to consult it? perhaps a TV presenter, building, through the happy photographs, the tragic voyage of a doomed ship. Such a narrator could also have another picture of Ruth as a young girl writing to her father about the wonderful ship. You might have considered two Ruths then—one coming from the happy family photograph and pushing her brother in a stroller, another, quieter Ruth writing to her father. This could have led you to wonder whether Ruth's father could have received her letter and so his Indian background could have been shown. You might even have had ideas about ship's stewards remembering that particular family as they proudly contemplate a reconstruction of a table set for dinner on the *Titanic*.

The second text is obviously in the style of one telling a story, explaining in fine detail some unusual events that have happened earlier; a minstrel with a lute, or a modern storyteller with a guitar, surrounded by people who can make all the sounds he or she introduces? Did you consider that the actors might also have become sheep? You might have thought of lots of different times when stories *have* to be told—perhaps to artists who are designing a tapestry?— The actors could form tableaux as the artists "draw" in the details or form swift "sculptures" as the tale unfolds.

There are some interesting locations in this tale, so you will probably have pondered how to move people around to indicate oak copse, the village, the haying boys, and the wolf-pit. Also, how many people you would like to introduce in addition to the shepherd and the two strange children?

There is another factor. This tale has been chronicled as accurate by two historians writing in the twelfth century, so it could be narrated by a traveling preacher or actors to country folks who might be astonished and terrified by the visitation of strange beings and hints of necromancy.

Whatever alternatives you have considered will have led you to a very close scrutiny of the texts, and you might have been pleasantly surprised by the number and variety of ideas you had. We hope so. This kind of thing definitely grows on you.

Appendix D
Pronounciation Guide for
King Arthur of England

We have used a simple respelling system except for the letter ə which conveys the sound represented by er in matt**er** or the a in **a**pprove. A line over a letter ‾ lengthens the sound.

Agravaine.	Ágrəvayn
Aldwulf.	Áldwo͞olf.
Bedwyr	Bédweer
Bernician	Berníssiən
Caledrwlch	Kalédrewlk.
Camlann	Kámlan
Cei	Sī́
Ceincaled	Sī́inkáaled.
Cerdic.	Chérdik.
Dunn Fionn	Dun Fée͘on
Eirlín	Áyrlin.
Gwalchmai.	Gwálkmī̄
Gwynhwyfar	Gwinwífə
Innsi Erc	Insi Érk
Lot of Orcade	Lot əf Áwkàdi.
Lugh	Lo͞og
Medraut	Médrawt
Morgawse	məgáwss
Rhys ap Sion	Riss ap Sśī̄ən.
Teilesan	Tī́leesən
Uther Pendragon.	Oothə Pendrágən

219